ESSENTIAL ADVICE FOR BUYING YOUR FIRST HOME AND NAVIGATING THROUGH THE MORTGAGE LOAN PROCESS

ANSWERS TO FIRST-TIME HOME BUYER QUESTIONS AND CONCERNS IN AN EASY-TO-FOLLOW 7-STEP GUIDE TO HOME BUYING

DIANA DONNELLY

DIANA DONNELLY

Disclaimer Regarding Financial Advice:

Before we embark on this journey to find a new house, it is important to note that the information contained in this book is not intended to be and must not be understood as a substitute for financial advice from a professional who has knowledge of the facts of your individual circumstances. This book is intended for general educational and informational purposes only, and the author cannot be held responsible for financial decisions that you may make that depend on your personal circumstances. The content of this book must not be understood as a suggestion not to conduct your own research or seek financial advice from a professional based on your specific situation before making financial decisions.

BONUS 3

Want this bonus book for FREE? Get access to this exclusive book and future books by joining my newsletter CLICK HERE TO JOIN or for print book scan below.

A SPECIAL GIFT TO OUR READERS

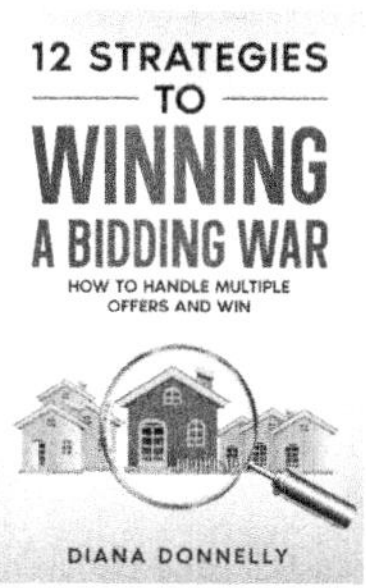

Included with the purchase of this book are ***The Strategies To Win Your House If You Are In A Bidding War booklet.*** These tips will help you to make a successful offer to win the bidding war . You can use this link to get your free copy https://bookhip.com/BQZPFZL.

INTRODUCTION

You worked hard and feel confident you are ready to buy your first home. Buying your first house is probably the most expensive purchase you will make in your lifetime. The problem is now that you feel you are ready, you need to prepare so you do everything correctly. You want to find the right house and get the right mortgage with the best interest rate. You need to be prepared and know the process before you move forward.

My daughter is at this same point in her life, and it's scary. She does have me to help her along the way, but not everyone has this type of guidance. It's a big decision; you can't just close on your house and walk away from it the next day if you change your mind. The last thing you want is to be overwhelmed working with a realtor and starting a mortgage application. There are discussions about money and there will be new terms that people throw at you. Are you ready to do this? You can see the benefits and want them - tax breaks, appreciation, and the feeling that this is your property and you can make it your own. Having your own home will give you a sense of security.

On the other hand, you are thinking, would it be so bad to rent and have someone else fix anything that might go wrong with your rental? Better yet, stay longer with your parents, and have a lot more disposable cash and a free meal. Once you use all or a good portion of your savings to purchase a home, it's not as easy to change jobs or move to a new place or even travel as much without such a significant financial burden.

The point of this book is to provide you with as much knowledge as possible to make the right decisions. Yes, buying a house is stressful, but it is also very gratifying and can provide you with security in the future. No more living with your parents, renting an apartment, dealing with a landlord, and having no control over who is above or below you. You can even have a pet if you want, as you make the rules.

You will understand the following after reading this book:

Be able to decide to purchase or keep renting for a while.

Find the best house in the best neighborhood for you. Be aware of the types of houses you can purchase. Decide if you want to buy a single- family house, a condominium, a townhouse, or maybe you want to buy something that you can rent out and have income potential to offset your mortgage payments.

Pick the best team to help you along the way. You will need to find a real estate agent, mortgage company, a home inspection company and a title company.

Understand the basic terms, documents, and costs involved with getting a mortgage.

Be able to decide what type of mortgage you will want and how much purchasing power you have.

Find the best house for your budget. Understand how to negotiate to get the best purchase price.

Know what steps you need to take to close on your new home and not be surprised by any of the fees involved with the closing.

Finally, arrange for your move and settle into your new home.

It feels incredible to be handed your keys knowing you are walking into your own home.

With over 30 years of experience in various real estate positions, I have the knowledge to provide you with advice on the home buying process. I started with my real estate license and a position working for a relocation company where I counseled employees and assisted them in their relocation around the country. If the employee could not sell their home before moving, I would arrange for an appraisal, and the company would purchase their home from them to give them enough funds to buy a new home in their new location. Once the company purchased the employee's home, I listed it and worked with an agent to market it until the home sold. I also prepared closing documents when the company purchased the home from the employee. I set up the employees on house hunting tours with well qualified realtors who really knew the area they were relocating to. In addition, I assisted the employee through finding a mortgage, interim housing, and finally moving.

After working in the relocation industry, I moved on to work for a mortgage company and now have 19 years of experience in this industry. I started processing loan documents and ran my own company for years. I changed my position from mortgage processing, and I am now a mortgage underwriter working for an incredible company in Virginia. In this position, I review borrower documents for accuracy and completeness and ensure the loan meets all guidelines for loan approval so the borrower can close. I am surrounded by family and friends that underwrite mortgages, sell real estate, appraise homes, and research and prepare title work for title companies.

One of the reasons I decided to write this book is to help my children have something they can refer to when they are ready to make this important step. I also realized this information can be valuable to others in the same situation. My advice comes from a knowledge of all areas of home purchase, and I have a passion for helping everyone achieve the ultimate goal of owning their first home.

STEP 1 : HOUSE AND LOCATION

WHY BUY A HOUSE?

Other than living with your parents rent-free, you will need to decide whether you want to rent a house or apartment or buy a house of your own. Consider the benefits of renting:

- All you pay every month is your rent, renters insurance, and utilities.
- If you are on a month-to-month lease, you can move to wherever you want to go as often as you like.
- No responsibility for any repairs or maintenance.

- Rent is typically less than what you would pay for your monthly mortgage payment.
- The security deposit for a rental is much less than saving a large deposit for a house.
- There are instances utility bills can even be included in the rent itself.
- You don't have to pay real estate or school taxes.

The downside of renting

- Amenities (appliances and general features) in the property will usually be older.
- All the money you spend on rent is just gone.
- You can't make any personal changes to the space without permission from your landlord. If repairs are needed, you must coordinate this with your landlord, and often times, wait.
- If you rent an apartment, you may have tenants above, below, or on either side of you. They could be loud and cause a lack of peace and privacy.
- The landlord can also decide to sell the property or raise the rent, making it unaffordable for you to stay there. Rental prices have increased in 50 of the largest metropolitan areas to an annual rate of 19.8% as of January 2022. Eight months in a row showed rising

rental prices reading a median of $1,789 per month. These statistics were based on studios, one-bedroom, and two-bedroom apartments (Settembre 2022).

Advantages to buying your own home

- If you choose a fixed-rate mortgage. The interest rate stays the same over the life of the loan. The payment consisting of principal and interest will be the same every month. If you have a conventional loan and have Private Mortgage Insurance (PMI) you can reduce your payment when your loan to value reaches 80%. Other costs may change annually, such as taxes and insurance costs.
- Owning your own home can provide you with stability. It can give you a sense of permanence and a place to make memories while growing your family.
- Your home is an investment in your future. Each time you pay your mortgage, you pay down the amount you owe on the house and build equity. Equity is the difference in the value of the home against the amount of the loan that you owe on the house. Once you pay off your mortgage, you only pay taxes and insurance. A great investment considering you

live in your asset. There are some exceptions, such as having an interest-only mortgage where you would not be paying off any of the principal.

- You can borrow against your home, as the equity increases, for home improvements or for other expenses you need to cover. You would do this with either a fixed second mortgage or a home equity line of credit (HELOC). The interest rates on this type of loan are typically higher than the rate on your first mortgage but are less than what you would pay on your credit cards.
- Owning a home can provide you with tax advantages. Each year a homeowner can write off their mortgage interest and property tax payment if itemizing. Schedule A of your tax return is where you would list things that you itemize. Note that the tax law changed in 2018. The amount you can itemize is now capped at $10,000. You can refer to your tax advisor for more information about this. Tax credits are also available if you buy energy-efficient products like solar or wind-generated electricity.
- The home you own is yours, and you can make whatever changes you want, i.e., remodel, paint, or decorate. In some instances, there may be

limitations from a homeowner association or historical guidelines.

- No rules on owning pets.
- You have all the privacy you want.
- When you buy a home, you also become part of the community.
- Your home can appreciate (meaning that your home can be worth more over time). The values can rise and fall but typically keep up with, or exceeds inflation. Appreciation is helpful because if you want to sell your house or move, you can use the equity you built to buy another home. When owning a home, you want your home to appreciate. There are two types of appreciation: market appreciation and forced appreciation.

Market Appreciation: This is how the home value appreciates over time. Many factors contribute to how high your value will increase.

1. Location: Most important factor. The value of the land will appreciate more than the value of the house. Homes near urban areas appreciate more than homes in rural areas. Community development of parks and walking trails will contribute to appreciation. Other factors

discussed in the next chapter will play a role in home values increasing.

2. Supply and Demand: The amount of homes for sale vs. the number of buyers seeking a home will have a major role in home appreciation. 2022 is an example of how supply and demand can increase values. Real estate markets across the country are reporting price gains up 15.7% from one year ago. In the Northeast, values increased by 6.7%, South by 20.1%, Midwest by 8.5%, and West by 5.9%. These increases have been happening at unprecedented rates for the past two years (Simmons, 2022). With the house prices soaring, you want to ask yourself if now is a good time for a first-time home buyer to be entering the housing market. Most experts feel it is still a good time to buy. Some feel that if prices are still increasing, you will gain equity, but if they lose some value when the market stabilizes, you pay less in taxes. Inflation seems to rise every month, which may scare you, but your assets will also gain value. As land is a limited commodity, your real estate values will increase.
3. Real estate comparable values: If values in your community increase, houses similar to your house will also appreciate.

4. The house with more usable square footage will be valued higher.
5. Zoning restrictions can affect your home value.
6. A healthy economy will help your home value. The desire to purchase a home will increase as more people have job stability.
7. Local, state, and federal tax policies or incentives can influence interest rates. Consumer confidence can be affected.
8. A natural or artificial disaster in one area can increase property values in unaffected areas.

Forced Appreciation: This type of appreciation will happen when the owner of the house makes improvements to the property. Improving curb appeal, which means making the outside of your house look good with things such as landscaping, walkways, new doors or windows, or adding bathrooms, bedrooms, or additional square feet, will increase the value of your home. Opendoor.com looked at different home products and ranked them for the increase in average value:

- Adding a pool 7.3% increase; resale increase $22,000
- Finishing a basement: 6.6% increase; resale increase $22,000
- Add a 3rd bedroom: 6.2% increase; resale increase$20,000

- Add full bathroom: 5.7% increase; resale increase $18,000
- Add living space: 5.3% increase; resale increase$17,000
- Full kitchen remodel: 4.8% increase; resale increase $15,000
- Converting existing square footage to a second or third bedroom: 4.3% increase; resale increase $14,000
- Full bathroom remodel: 3.7% increase; resale increase $11,000
- Install hardwood flooring: 3.4% increase; resale increase $10,000
- Add a half bathroom; 2.9% increase; resale increase $9,000
- Add an attached garage: 2.2% increase; resale increase by $7,000 (Marino & Gomez, 2019).

Disadvantages of Home Ownership

- Coming up with a large down payment to purchase the home.
- Mortgage payments are typically higher than rental payments. You will have to pay monthly property taxes and homeowners insurance. Some states have separate school taxes. The costs of these can increase annually.

- Buying a home is typically a longer commitment.
- You need to be prepared if you have to replace a big-ticket item like a roof. Especially if you buy an older home or fixer-upper. Be prepared by putting money into a home maintenance fund. You'll be glad you did it.

Nerdwallet.com has a rent vs. buy calculator that is helpful. The calculator can help you see the costs of living differences in the areas you are thinking of living. To use the calculator, you would need to input six key pieces of information:

1. The area where you think you may want to live.
2. The estimate of what you would think the purchase price would be.
3. What your down payment would be.
4. The length of time for your mortgage. Typically 30 years
5. An estimate of the length of time you intend to live there
6. An estimate of what you believe the cost would be to rent a home similar to the one you want to purchase.

https://nerdwallet.com/mortgages/rent-vs-buy-calculator.

There is no right or wrong answer to whether or not you should buy a home. Buying your first home is a choice based on your preference of what is best for you. If it is the right time to purchase, your financial situation will play a big part in the timing.

Studies show that one of the biggest concerns of a first-time home buyer is a fear of a significant drop in the new home's value causing negative equity. Current market conditions compared to market conditions in 2008 are very different. In 2022 there will be no housing bubble. A housing bubble occurs when prices rise quickly due to increased demand and spending. It starts with an increase in demand when there is a limited supply. Investors add money into the market and make the demand even higher. Then over time, the demand will decrease, and supply will increase, causing a significant drop in prices and the bubble to burst. In the early 2000s, investors made investments in the housing market combined with loose lending conditions and a government policy to increase home ownership. When the value of homes declined, many homeowners defaulted on their loans. At that time, lenders were making risky loans without checking a borrower's information to confirm the income and assets on the loan application were valid. Many loans were "no income, no asset loans." In this type of loan, the lender receives a loan application that includes the basic information about the borrower. The borrower listed where they worked but did not list how much money they made in their job or how much money they had in savings to buy the house, and nothing was verified. Mortgage loans changed in the early 2000s to ensure this would not happen again. When you apply for a mortgage now, lenders will verify that you are making enough money to afford your house and prove where your funds are coming from to pay for the home. Homeowners in 2022 have built a large amount of equity as values appreciate. You can protect yourself by paying market value for the property and making sure you make smart purchase decisions. Try to save and have a larger down payment. If you plan to be in your house for an extended period and can afford to pay a little extra toward your mortgage payment, this will increase your equity faster and decrease the total amount you pay over the the life of the loan. Another concern of the first-time home buyer is keeping up with the amount of down payment to buy a house when the values are rising at unprecedented rates. If the average appreciation of homes in your area increases by 3%, you should try to increase the amount you are saving for a down payment by 3%. It will be essential to try and budget and just continue to save toward your goal. Chapter 3 discusses budgeting and costs to expect with purchasing and new home. Chapter 5 provides different mortgage options to help you afford a home with less money.

TYPES OF HOUSES & IMPORTANCE OF LOCATION

Location

Where do you want to put down roots, and what factors should you consider? A lot more people are working remotely in 2022, giving more options for places to settle down. A list of things to consider:

Cost of Living: It's more than just the house. Some areas are more expensive to live in than others. It is higher when living in or near a large city than in a small town. Make sure you consider the cost of groceries, durable goods, transportation, and health care. Use a cost of living calculator to compare different areas. https://bestplaces.net/cost-of-living/. This calculator will let you compare the prices of other regions of the United States. To give you an idea of the information provided by the calculator, it states that if the cost of living index has a rank of 135, then it is 35% more expensive than the national average cost of living. The lower the cost of living rank, the closer it is to the nation's average location (*2022 Cost of Living Calculator*, n.d.).

Taxes are an essential consideration- Some states don't charge sales taxes: Oregon, Montana, New Hampshire, Alaska, and Delaware. You can also look at states that have no income tax. The following map shows how income taxes are broken down in each state: (Vermeer And Loughead, 2022).

Other taxes to consider are property taxes, school taxes (even if you don't have children), gasoline taxes, and business taxes and fees. There is a large difference between real estate/property taxes in New Jersey and Illinois compared to Alabama and Hawaii. Some states provide homestead exemptions where a homeowner is protected from excessive taxation. Zillow.com has a chart that looks at the average median price of single-family homes and annual property taxes by state. You can view this chart to see how the state you are interested in buying compares to other locations by clicking this line to WalletHub (Rohde, 2022b).

Employment Opportunity: The differences in salaries paid around the country vary widely. There has been an increase in the number of people working remotely. Working from home provides new opportunities to move anywhere you like but ensure you understand if your salary will be the same or if it will go up or down. Salaries for companies located in larger cities would tend to be higher than salaries in remote areas.

Crime Rates: Ideally, you would want to look for a low crime rate location. You want to feel safe where you buy your home. A website https://areavibes.com/can help you find areas with low crime rates. It presents a livability score to help you find where to live based on ratings; local amenities, cost of living, crime, employment, housing, and schools.

Real Estate Values: Real estate values are constantly changing. Research the current home prices, how long homes are listed for sale, are these homes selling above what they are listed for or below this price. You can use websites like Trulia, Redfin, and Zillow to aid you.

Family and Friends: A big consideration is how far you want to move from family and friends. It can be isolating to move far away and miss out on socializing with close friends and family. It can also be expensive and time-consuming to travel to see everyone. It is nice to be near family if you have young children for support and assistance.

Climate: The climate in the area you decide to live in is important for your quality of life. If you hate the winter and snow shoveling, moving to Buffalo, NY, would not be the place for you. Maybe you like the beach and want to be in warm sunny areas or live in Arizona, known for its clean air that is good for your lungs.

Activities: It's important to surround yourself with a community that offers activities in which you are interested. Regarding recreational activities, you may want to live near ski resorts if you are an avid skier. For those who love to be close to fine arts a community with ready access to museums, music events, and theaters may be best for you. Being near a larger city would give you many fine dining and entertainment options.

Education and Schools: For families with children or who are intending on having children, the school system can be one of the biggest deciding factors in where you want to settle. Home prices are typically higher in better school districts and a choice you need to make. You can research school systems by visiting nonprofit websites like https://schooldigger.com/ and https://greatschools.org/. If you can afford private school rather than public school this may not be as big of a deciding factor.

Commute: Even though many people are working from home, there remains a large population of the work-force still commuting to work. The amount of time spent commuting or sitting in traffic can take away valuable time you could spend on other things. Give careful consideration to this, as you may want to consider access to public transportation or living within a certain mile radius of your place of employment.

Health Care: Having great healthcare nearby is an important to consideration. You want to be near good and reliable hospitals if you have children, have a chronic health condition, or are near retirement age. Major cities or towns near universities would have more choices in hospitals and prominent research universities than if you went to a more rural area.

Airports: Living close to an airport is important if you have to commute for business often or if you love to travel. Getting flights out of smaller regional airports can be difficult, and if you live far away, you need to consider the additional travel time it would take to get to and from the airport. It can also be expensive to get a car service to take you to the airport if you live far away.

RESALE VALUE

Your house is one of your most significant financial investments, so you should strongly consider resale value. You need to determine if you will have to make a large cash investment to improve the value.

- Make sure to buy your house at the best price possible. You can do this by doing some research in advance of your offer.
- Look to check the curb appeal of the house. It should look like everything is well taken care of and has a nice entryway.
- If the house you are looking at is the highest price on the block, you need to check that it has more supported features as the competition in the neighborhood to support the increased value. It is good if your house is the least expensive in the area but is surrounded by higher-value homes as that will increase the value.
- As mentioned above, the school system is very important to look at. It is one of the first things parents with school-age children look for. What is the quality of the local schools? Houses are valued higher in a highly rated school district.

- Neighborhood plays another role in value. Many people would like to live in a relaxing, peaceful area. Living near trains or busy highways creates a lot of noise and may reduce values.
- Proximity to amenities also factor into the house value. Many want to be close to dining, shopping, and recreation. If your house is close to desirable destinations, that is a plus.
- The safety of the neighborhood will make a difference in value.
- A family-friendly house typically is more desirable. This is a house that has three or more bedrooms. They sell for a higher price and faster than a one or two-bedroom house. Having more than one bathroom is another amenity valued by the homebuyer.
- A house in great shape: Buyers want well kept and maintained houses that will not require major repairs. This is especially important for a first-time home buyer as roof issues, HVAC Systems, wiring, and plumbing can be big-ticket items to repair.
- Storage: It is good to pay attention to what kind of storage the house has. Does it have enough places to store not only your cars but, sports gear, bicycles, lawn and garden tools, etc? Does the house have enough spaces to store clothes

and kitchen items? Houses with ample storage are appealing to home buyers.

- Homes on the market: If there are fewer homes for people to choose from, the housing value will increase. For example, the pandemic caused people to stop selling houses in early 2022. The pandemic caused a nationwide low inventory level of housing. There is also a shortage of new homes being built. Millennials are between the ages of 23-41. They are the largest living generation in the United States. Research has shown that this generation does not have as high homeownership as past generations. Research has shown that out of 10 home buyers, more than four buyers fall into this generation. 2022 housing trends show that those on the older end of generation Z are experiencing a tight housing inventory as the number of affordable homes continues to be limited (LaPonsie, 2022). With current inventory so low, sellers are getting top dollar for their houses.
- Check for neighborhood rules: It can be helpful to have a neighborhood that has a homeowners association (HOA) as the association makes rules and monitors the homes to make sure the values of all the homes are not reduced by local homeowners not taking care of their property

or keeping broken down cars in their driveway or street.

- The size of the lot: Bigger lots can be a plus for many buyers as it gives them space between their home and the neighbors and allows them to do outdoor entertaining or garden. Where the house is located on the street, such as at the end of the street on a cul-de-sac, can be valued more than in other areas of the street.
- Upgrades: If you are looking at a house in a development, many of them look the same. Adding amenities inside the house, like upgraded kitchen countertops and flooring, can increase the value and appeal to someone looking at buying the home.

HOUSES TO AVOID

Resale value is important when looking for a new home. Try to avoid purchasing houses near:

Busy streets/highways- Try to avoid houses near busy streets and highways. This can have a negative impact, as people worry about noise and safety. Especially families with children or pets. It also could cause issues with having a place to park if your house does not have a driveway and you need to park on the street.

Railroad Tracks-The loud noise from trains and safety concerns if you live close to a rail line can cause values to be less.

Power Lines- Try to avoid being near power lines. The house price will be more affordable, there will be less competition for the house, and you probably will not need to pay homeowners association fees. Studies show that houses near power lines will have lower property values. The power lines are not aesthetically pleasing, and people worry about health-related issues. There are concerns that the radiation from the power lines can cause cancer, but there are no research studies to prove this concern. There may also be restrictions on your property that you need to worry about if you want to make any landscaping changes. If you're very close to power lines. You may have to listen to loud humming noises constantly.

Flat Roof-A flat roof gives you extra space to use as an outdoor area and is easier to maintain. This sounds like a great option; however, the larger the flat roof area, the more the roof's stability decreases. A flat roof has a limited lifespan, and they have many drainage problems. Water tends to puddle and stay on the roof, which erodes the roofing materials and can cause leaks. A flat roof is not a good option in a location where you will get large amounts of snow. The weight of the snow could cause issues with the roof's stability.

An unusual house-The home may appeal to your taste, but living in a unique home can negatively impact your resale value. Not everyone will want a house like this.

WHAT IS THE RIGHT HOUSE FOR ME?

Start by thinking about who is going to live in the house. Will it just be you on your own, or are you going to have a roommate or a tenant with you? Do you need to consider the needs of one child or multiple? Do you think you may have an elderly parent live with you? Do you have a pet that will need outdoor space? The number of bedrooms and bathrooms will be important. Also, if you have small children and elderly relatives, think about how well they could handle going up and down the stairs.

Would the house fit your lifestyle now and in the future? Before you agree to buy what you think might be your dream house, consider your long-term plans. Are you planning on staying at your current job? Getting married? Having kids? If you are working or plan to work at home, you would want space for a home office. If you are just thinking about purchasing a house to fit your current needs maybe you want a smaller house.

Many people now use their homes to make extra income by renting out rooms on sites like HomeAway,

VRBO, and Airbnb. "Airbnb hosts make, on average, about $924 a month, according to research from low-interest lender Earnest"(Leonhardt, 2019). This amount varies based on where your home is located and what services you offer. If you decided to do something like this, you would need the room layout to work to give you enough privacy and have someone in your home. You also need to consider that you will now be both a landlord and a roommate.

If you found a house with an apartment over the garage or a basement area with a separate entrance, you can do a long-term rental. This extra money every month will offset the cost of your mortgage.

Another option is to consider a multi-family property. A multi-family is a property that has two to four units.

This allows you to buy your own home and have tenants pay part or all of the mortgage payment. It's a place for you to live and enables you to build wealth at the same time.

A multi-family can be a duplex with two separate units. A triplex has three separate units, and a fourplex with four separate units. Each unit will have a separate entrance, kitchen, and bathrooms. You can have tax breaks when you own investment units. If you live in one of the units, you would purchase this property as your primary residence and not an investment property. You would qualify the same as purchasing a single-family property. The difference is that 75% of the rent the other units in the property generate can count toward your income for loan qualification. As property value increases and you use the rental income to pay your mortgage, you are building equity in your house faster than if you purchased a single-family home. There could also be a drawback of the multi-family property as you have to find renters and not only manage the tenants but live with them at the same time.

TYPES OF HOMES YOU CAN PURCHASE

There are many types and styles of homes to choose from. Would you want an older home or a newer

home? You can look for homes in developments or individual neighborhoods where you would not pay a fee to belong to a Homeowner Association.

The single-family home: This home type is not connected to any other building. The homeowner owns both the house and the land it is on. They come in various styles:

-Ranch style: This home type is all on one level. Many have an attached garage with a large picture window and sliding doors leading to the backyard. Some can be a raised ranch with a basement level that is on ground level and has a door leading out to the yard.

-Cape Cod style: This was originally designed in the New England area to be able to protect against the harsh winters. The homes have shutters that could be closed to protect the windows and keep out the cold. The original homes featured a central fireplace, but now they can be located anywhere in the home. This home type usually has one or one and a half stories with a steep roof and small overhang. It has a symmetrical appearance with a center door and dormers with windows.

-Victorian style: Originated between 1830 to 1900 and can be called Queen Anne. The homes usually have intricate woodwork and feature a large wraparound porch. In the past, they were painted in bright colors

and had verandas, turrets, and many multi-purpose rooms for large families. The interior of many of these houses has high ceilings and many archways with small rooms for different uses.

-Colonial Style: Originated on the east coast to be able to handle the cold and rough weather. Many offer a central fireplace and low ceilings for retaining heat. The colonists were from various countries and brought their styles with them, which is why there is a subset of styles: Georgian, Dutch, and Spanish. These homes are symmetrical. They are typically 2-3 stories with a rectangular shape, and some have decorative crown molding with large living areas on the first floor and bedrooms on the second.

-Tudor Style: This style originated in England and has multi-gabled roofs that are steeply pitched and have large chimneys and small dormers. They have large narrow windows with many panes.

-Mediterranean Style: This style has its background in Greece, Spain, and Italy. They usually have a stucco exterior with large arched windows and red clay roof tiles. Many have large outdoor living areas with verandas or balconies

-Contemporary/Modern Style: This type of home is usually built with ecologically friendly materials and features clean lines and textures.

-Modern Farmhouse: A relatively new style that has features of a traditional farmhouse but has high ceilings, large front porches, and exposed beams. They mix the clean lines of the contemporary house with the simple style of a farmhouse.

-Prairie Style: It is designed to embrace the environment around the home. It gained its popularity from Frank Lloyd Wright. This style has an open floor plan and features simple natural woodwork

-Mid-Century Modern: Like the prairie style, this home is designed to integrate nature and has straight lines, open spaces, and large glass windows. Some have a bi-level floor plan. They focus on floor-to-ceiling windows and open floor plans

-Split-Level: A type of ranch-style home that started in the 1950s. Short flights of stairs separate two living spaces.

-Cottage Style: Usually cozy smaller homes with small porches and fireplaces.

-French Country Style: Designed after homes found in the French countryside. They usually have pointed roofs and shutters with stone on the outside and feature natural materials

-Bungalow Style: This style has variations depending on the area-California style, Michigan style, or Chicago style. Usually has stone elements with one or one and a half stories and large covered front porches. It has built-in shelving and cabinets as well as a large fire-place. The living room is usually in the center of the house.

-Craftsman Style: This home has many hand-crafted wood features, exposed beams, and tapered columns on the porches.

Semi-Detached Home: This single-family home is attached to another home by one wall. Typically the floor plan is the same for each house.

Multi-family Homes: This house has more than one housing unit. Each unit has a separate entrance, bathroom, and kitchen area.

Townhomes: This style has multiple floors. The house shares walls on both sides unless it is the end unit. Many are part of a homeowners association where you would pay a fee for the association to maintain the common areas outside.

Condominiums (Condos): This is a building style where the unit inside the building is owned. They seem similar to apartment buildings. You own and maintain the interior space, but the condominium association takes care of the common area. Many offer amenities, such as a gym or pool in the common area.

Co-Ops: This style looks like an apartment, but anyone that buys this style is purchasing as a shareholder. The shareholders have a corporation that owns and manages the building.

Tiny Home: This is a recently popular style of home that is no more than 400 square feet in size.

Mobile/Manufactured Home: This style home is a manufactured home. It is built in a factory and has a permanent chassis with wheels. They typically are no larger than 2200 square feet.

Modular Home: This style is a manufactured home built in a factory until it is about 80-90% complete and then sent by truck in different pieces and put together on the site. They come with a builder warranty and appreciate the same as a site-built house.

There are many variables to consider when viewing homes. Creating a list of what you may or may not want in your new home can be helpful when starting the search. Write down all of the features that you absolutely must have in a home like the number of bedrooms, bathrooms, style of house, size of the house, how many stories high, basement or no basement, what kind of neighborhood you want to be in and other things, like how big of a yard you would want. Additional features include a first floor or second floor laundry room, deck, pool, garage, fireplace, flooring, type of parking, and fenced yard. Make a list of the amenities you want to have in your kitchen. When you go out and look at houses, you can compare them to your purchasing list. Don't forget to put things like central air, storage, neighborhood, and school system ratings on the list.

SPECIAL BONUS

FREE planner to help you document your purchase. Get access to this and all of my new books by joining my newsletter CLICK HERE TO JOIN for ebook or scan below if you have a print book

STEP 2 : FINANCES & CREDIT

MANAGING YOUR FINANCES

Many mortgage lenders will review your income and suggest you can afford payments from 28% of housing-related costs, including mortgage, insurance, and taxes, to a ⅓ of your gross income each month. You may want to get a mortgage that is the most you can qualify for, but that may not be the amount of additional debt you would want to handle every month.

Look beyond the purchase price: When buying a new home, it's important to know the costs involved in the transaction. There are many more expenses than the down payment. Many of the expenses, especially the down payment is related to the purchase price of the home. In 2022 home sales prices are skyrocketing. The median home price in America was $392,000. It increased from $305,000 in 2021. This home price includes newly built and existing homes combined. (Ramsey Solutions, 2022).

COSTS BEYOND THE PURCHASE PRICE

- Your Deposit: The earnest money deposit is the first cost you will need to consider. This is typically 1% to 3% of the purchase price. Placing this deposit lets the seller know you are committing to purchase the home. If you are purchasing new construction the seller may want a 10% earnest money deposit. Based on the median home price of $392,000, the earnest money deposit would be $3,920 or $39,200 for new construction. If competing with many other buyers, you may consider making a higher earnest money deposit to stand out from the other buyers. Your realtor can advise you what would be the typical amount needed for your area and current market conditions. This money is paid to either your real estate agency or your chosen title company/attorney you have chosen. It is held in an escrow account (this is an account set up where only the earnest money deposits of clients can be placed) and cannot be touched until all terms of the purchase agreement are met. You can lose this money to the seller if you do not hold up your end of the contract, or you can back out and get the money back if the seller does not live up to the terms of the sales contract. If the sale continues without problems, this money will go toward your down payment and closing costs.

- Down Payment: This is part of the sales price you will need to pay for the house not covered by your mortgage. The more money you put down on the house, the better. Typical loan programs are conventional loans where you put down a minimum of 3% of the sales price; FHA loans, where you would put down 3.5% of the sales price. VA loans (loans for Veterans) and USDA loans do not require any down payment. If you get a jumbo loan (a loan higher than the standard conventional loan limit), it would be 10% to 20% of the sale price.
- The seller can give you a credit of up to 3% of the sales price if your loan to value (the loan amount divided by your house's sales price, also known as LTV) exceeds 90%. If your LTV is anywhere from 75.01% to 90%, the maximum allowed is 6% closing cost credit. If your LTV is 75% or less, the seller can credit up to 9% of

your closing costs. On an FHA loan, the limit paid toward closing costs can go up to 6%, and on VA loans, it can be up to 4% of the sales price. Of course, this would have to be negotiated and included in the sales contract. If you are competing with many other buyers in a hot market, getting a seller to agree to contribute toward your closing costs would be difficult. The closing costs covered cannot be more than the closing costs themselves.

- Closing Costs: Fees you will need to pay when you settle on your home. They vary based on location and what type of loan you are taking out. The average cost can run between two percent and five percent of the loan amount. Later chapters will discuss the closing costs in more detail.

BUDGETING FOR YOUR COSTS AND MONTHLY MORTGAGE PAYMENTS

Buying a home requires saving and spending a large amount of money. Before you head out the door to begin the house search, you want to have enough savings to cover the down payment and the closing costs. Traditionally it's good to have 20% of the purchase price as your down payment. It's optimal to put as much money down for your down payment to make a competitive offer and reduce the size of your mortgage. Different loans allow you to put down different amounts. Also, if you put down less than 20% of the purchase price, you will be required to purchase private mortgage insurance, which could increase your monthly mortgage payment. There are loan programs where you can put much less money down and a large majority of borrowers do not put the full 20%. The National Association of Realtors (NAR) analyzed the purchase trends throughout the United States. The NAR found that based on the home's value, the average down payment among all buyers was 12%, with an average of three years of saving up. (Warden, 2021)

NAR further broke the average down payment on a home by age group:

All Buyers: 12%

Age 22-30: 6%

Age 31-40: 10%

Age 41-55: 13%

Age 56-65: 18%

Age 66-74: 23%

Age 95-95: 21%

(Warden, 2021)

CREATING A BUDGET

Regardless of which type of mortgage you choose, you will need some money at closing, even for a no-down-payment mortgage. There are many costs other than just the closing costs. You also need to consider moving costs and the money you will want to spend on decorating. Creating a budget can help you plan for these expenses. Having a budget helps you know what you are spending your money on and where you can cut back on areas that will help you save. Many websites have budget calculators to help you, such as www.youneedabudget.com.

Review Your Expenses

Once you have your budget put together, review your expenses to see how much money you feel you can pay each month toward your mortgage payment. You may make enough money to qualify for a higher mortgage than you feel you can comfortably pay. The last thing you need is to get into a situation where you stay awake at night worrying if you have the funds to pay the next monthly payment.

Qualifying

When the lender qualifies you for a mortgage, they base all their numbers on your gross pay. This is the amount of pay before any taxes are taken out. Your mortgage payment would be the entire payment (principal, interest, taxes, home insurance, private mortgage insurance, and, if you are buying in a community, a homeowners association fee). Lenders' typical guideline for qualifying is 28% of your gross pay, but this can vary and be higher depending on the loan program you apply for.

GIFT FUNDS

Many people use gifts to help with down payment and closing costs.

Who can give a gift? If you have a relative willing to help you, they are allowed to give you gift funds. Only relatives related by blood, marriage, guardianship, adoption, a domestic partner, or significant others like a fiancé can provide gift funds.

Guidelines for receiving a gift: The lender must verify that the money is a gift, not a loan. The gift donor and the borrower will sign a form to state this is true. If you are putting down 20% of the purchase price and purchasing a 1-4 unit single-family home or a second home, all the funds needed for closing can be from a gift. When you have a down payment of less than 20%, the rule is still the same for a 1-4 unit single-family home. All of the funds can be from a gift. The guidelines change if you buy a second home or 2-4 unit property and put down less than 20%. In this case, you would have to have 5% of your own money. For an FHA loan, gifts can be from family members or friends that can show a "clearly defined documented interest" in the buyer. FHA also allows for employers, labor unions, or charitable organizations to do a down payment gift. Gifts can be for up to 100% of the funds needed to close. You can still receive gifts for VA and USDA loans. These loan programs do not require a down payment, and there is no restriction on the amount of money you can be given as a gift.

What do you need to prove if you received a gift? There needs to be a paper trail of the gift coming from the donor to the borrower. It cannot be cash handed from the donor to the borrower. If you do receive a gift, you will need to show where the money came from by providing a copy of the canceled check (the front and back of the check after it is cashed) and show the funds deposited in your bank account. You can also provide a copy of the wire confirmation that shows the funds were wired from the donor to the borrower. The funds can be paid directly to the title company handling the closing. If the loan is an FHA loan, you will need the donor to provide a copy of their bank statement showing they can pay the gift.

USING YOUR 401 K

If you work for a company that has a 401K many of the plans allow you to make a withdrawal from what you have saved to buy a home. If you don't want to make a hardship withdrawal (the emergency removal of funds from your 401k plan), you can choose to take out a 401k loan and pay it back to yourself. This loan will not count as an additional monthly payment with the lender because you are paying back yourself, and it is not reported to a credit bureau.

CREDIT HISTORY

You may have seen some ads on tv or the radio from credit companies talking about your credit score. So what is your credit score? Your credit score shows how fiscally responsible you are with your debt. The score is based on a number from 300–850. If your scores are high creditors will want to lend to you. The credit agencies base your score on five factors:

1. Your payment history-This makes up the largest part of your score.
2. The length of time you have credit opened.
3. How much you utilize your credit.
4. Recent inquiries.
5. Diversification of credit.

When you start looking for a lender, you will want to check rates with various companies. Your credit score will not be affected by shopping for a mortgage rate even though you will have multiple inquiries so long as all inquiries are within a thirty-day window.

When a lender looks at your credit score, they are reviewing the likelihood of you paying their loan to you on time. The following are how the scores are considered:

Excellent: 800 to 850

Very Good: 740 to 799

Good: 670 to 739

Fair: 580 to 669

Poor: 300 to 579

(Investopedia Team, 2021)

CREDIT SCORE

Lenders and your credit: Lenders typically pull a credit report from three different companies, Experian, Equifax, and Transunion. When evaluating which score to use for a mortgage, a lender will look at all the borrower's scores and choose the one with the lowest middle score. Different loan types follow different credit score guidelines:

- Conventional Loan: Typically, a conventional loan will require a minimum credit score of 620, but some lenders may require higher scores.
- FHA Loan: A minimum credit score of 500 is allowed on an FHA loan, but you would have to put a 10% down payment instead of 3.5%. If you are doing the maximum financing with 3.5% down, your score would need to be 580 or above.
- VA Loan: There is no credit score requirement for a VA loan as the entire loan profile is reviewed.
- USDA Loan: USDA doesn't require a score, but they look to ensure the applicant can show they know how to handle and manage debt. It is best to have a 640 or higher score in this program.

THE CREDIT REPORT

Now that you know what lenders look for in a credit score, you should get a copy of your credit report from each of the three national credit bureaus. Equifax, Experian, and TransUnion. They allow you to do this for free on Annualcreditreport.com. Once you get a copy, you must review each and ensure the correct information is listed. Check what may be helping or hurting your score.

What is hurting my score? Your score will be lower if your report shows missed payments or payments made 30 or more days late, you have high credit card balances, collection accounts, or judgments.

What will improve my score? If your score is not where you want it to be, you can still improve it. If you have a lot of credit card debt, try to pay the card down so that your balance is at 30% of your credit limit. 10% utilization or less is the best. If you have mistakes on your credit report, try to get the credit bureaus to remove them. If you have collection accounts, delinquent accounts, or charge-offs, resolve them before buying a house. Many collection companies will negotiate to pay off the account.

If you don't have a credit history, some companies work with you to add your on-time rent payments and utility payments to your credit report.

A few options to look at are:

Extra Credit: credit.com/extracredit/

Rent Reporters: rentreporters.com

Simplebills: simplebills.com

You can also try to get a secured credit card to build up your credit history.

COLLECTION ACCOUNTS

A collection account will not stop you from being approved for a mortgage. Your loan program would depend on the type of bad credit and how much bad credit you have. If you have late child support payments, tax liens, or late student loan payments, they would need to be paid off or brought current to close on the loan. If you owe money to the IRS and can't pay off the full amount due, you can set up a payment plan

and show the lender that you have made payments on time. If you are having issues with your credit, it would be best to discuss it with a lender to find out how to deal with them.

BANKRUPTCY

You can still get a mortgage if you had a bankruptcy in the past. The lender will check when it was dismissed and want to see that you have re-established a positive payment history.

The most common types of bankruptcies are Chapter 7, Chapter 13, and Chapter 11:

- Chapter 7: This is most common for individuals. A court trustee will oversee the sale of your assets (items you own of value) that are not necessities like your house, retirement, or car. The funds from the sale pay off your creditors (anyone you owe money to). Any other debts that cannot be paid off are erased. You cannot forgive a student loan or taxes. That will still need to be paid. If you own a home, Chapter 7 cannot stop a foreclosure (where the bank takes your property for non-payment), but it can slow the process down. If you want to keep your property, you must agree to continue making mortgage payments (reaffirm the debt). The court only allows bankruptcy if you show you do not make enough money to pay off your debts. You will need to go to court to complete the bankruptcy and answer any questions that creditors may have. This type of bankruptcy will stay on your credit report for ten years.
- Chapter 13: A Chapter 13 bankruptcy reorganizes your debt. The court reviews all documentation and provides a payment plan so you can pay a portion of the unsecured debt and all of your secured debt back over three to five years. The court will put you on a strict spending budget. This bankruptcy will be able to stop a foreclosure and allows you to catch up

on paying your debt. This type of bankruptcy will stay on your credit report for seven years.

- Chapter 11: This type of bankruptcy reorganizes a debtor's business debts and assets. It is complex and allows a company to continue operating its business while reorganizing.

If you had a bankruptcy, lenders have a specific time frame for each loan type you would need to wait for before applying for a mortgage loan.

- Conventional loans: You would have to wait four years before you can apply for a mortgage for a Chapter 7 bankruptcy or Chapter 11 bankruptcy. It is a little different from Chapter 13 bankruptcy. In this instance, it is two years from when it was discharged or four years from when it was dismissed. If you have had more than one bankruptcy in the past seven years, you will need to wait five years.
- FHA Loan: On an FHA loan, you can apply two years after the discharge of a Chapter 7 bankruptcy and twelve months after a Chapter 13 discharge, but only if you made 12 months on time bankruptcy payments and have written permission from the bankruptcy court to get a new mortgage.

- USDA Loan: On a USDA loan, you would need to wait three years after a discharge or dismissal of a bankruptcy.
- VA Loan: VA requires a two-year wait period.

An important note on credit. When you start the loan process, your credit is pulled. It is rechecked before you close on your loan. If you go out and buy furniture, a car, or another large purchase before you close, this will show up on your credit. The lender will need to go back and add this debt to your other debts to ensure you still qualify for your loan. If you have an emergency and need to make a large purchase, discuss it with the lender to ensure it will not cause issues with your loan approval.

Credit Repair if needed

If your credit score is below 640, it will be harder to qualify for a good mortgage interest rate. If this is your situation, take the time in advance to improve your score. Some credit issues can be cleaned up quickly, whereas others may take a couple of years. When you get a copy of your credit report, check that the information is accurate. There are instances where you may be a victim of identity theft. Credit could have been taken out in your name, or possibly a creditor reported the wrong information on one of your charges. Not much anyone can do if the information on your credit is correct. Information will stay on the report for up to seven years. You have the right to dispute the information if it is incorrect.

To dispute erroneous credit information, the Federal Trade Commission (FTC) has a specific process you would need to follow. You need to write to each credit bureau that lists the error and attach copies of any documentation showing the mistake. Another option is to contact the creditor directly and provide them with the information to see if they will remove the mistake from your credit report. Once you supply your letter (also known as a 609 dispute letter) and documentation outlining the mistake, the law requires that the bureau look into the problem within 30 days (providing it makes sense). The bureau would also give this information to the credit company you are disputing. (D'Angelo, 2021).

The 609 dispute letter does not discuss your right to dispute the credit. It does claim your right to a copy of all the information in your credit file. The 609 letter is just another way of gathering information to dispute the items reported on the credit report. If disputes are successful, the credit bureaus may remove the negative item. Any accurate or verifiable information will stay on your credit report—a 609 letter doesn't guarantee removal. You can file your dispute online at each credit company: Experian, Equifax, and TransUnion.

When the investigation is completed, you will receive written notification of the outcome. If the result is in your favor, all credit bureaus need to be notified so files can be corrected. If not in your favor, you can still add a written explanation to have placed in your credit file.

You can also have the option to hire a company to handle the credit issues for you but be careful as there are a lot of scam companies. The Consumer Financial Protection Bureau lists some warning signs when looking at companies:

- No credit agency will be able to remove every derogatory credit item from your report. If a company claims this, it would be a warning sign.
- If the credit repair agency tells you to dispute correct information, it would be fraud and is another major red flag.
- If a credit repair company is legitimate, they will not ask for any money to be paid upfront. You can also sign up with a credit repair company and not have to pay fees if you cancel within three days (D'Angelo, 2021).

STEP 3 : THE MORTGAGE

QUALIFYING FOR THE MORTGAGE WHAT IS A MORTGAGE?

 mortgage is an agreement between a buyer and a lender that gives the lender the authority to take your property if you don't make the payments owed plus interest. The mortgage payment is made up of the following:

PITI:

Principal: The amount of money you pay each month that will pay down what you owe against the loan

Interest: The interest you pay each month on your loan

Taxes: The lender will collect monthly real estate taxes. As part of your loan payment, pay your taxes when they are due. You can opt-out of paying the taxes on your mortgage if you have a down payment of 20% or more.

Homeowners Insurance: The lender will collect monthly homeowners insurance payments as part of your mortgage payment and pay your homeowner's insurance company when the bill is due each year. You can opt-out of paying the taxes on your mortgage if you have a down payment of 20% or more.

The mortgage payment's taxes and homeowner insurance can change each year. It is the taxes and insurance that are escrowed. Escrowed means that the lender collects funds at closing to cover the first year annual payment and also in each mortgage payment to pay for your taxes and homeowners insurance bills as they come due in the following year. Typically the homeowner insurance will renew annually. Real estate taxes vary by state. Taxes can be due annually, semi-annually, or quarterly.

Private mortgage insurance can be added to the payment if you put a down payment of less than 20%:

Private Mortgage Insurance (PMI)

This is insurance that you pay on a conventional loan each month that protects the lender if you stop making payments on your loan. If you do not want this insurance as part of your mortgage payment, you can pay the entire fee upfront or do a combination of both.

MORTGAGE TERM

A mortgage term is the number of years your mortgage will last. When you decide to get a mortgage, you can choose different mortgage terms: The typical term of a loan is 30 years. Other options are a 40-year term, 25-year term; 20-year term; 15-year term, 10-year term, and a 5-year term. The shorter the term, the higher your principal and interest payment will be.

HOW SHOULD I CHOOSE A LENDER FOR MY MORTGAGE?

There are different types of mortgage professionals. There are retail lenders, direct lenders, mortgage lenders, mortgage brokers, correspondent lenders, wholesale lenders, and others that can a combination of the above.

The Mortgage Lender/Banker

A mortgage lender is a mortgage bank or company that can offer and underwrite loans. They have specific guidelines and set the terms of your mortgage. Lenders charge a fee for their services.

- Retail lender: Provide mortgages directly to the consumer. A retail lender would be a bank, credit union, and mortgage banker.
- Direct lenders: Originate their loan with their funds or borrow the funds from other sources. This type of lender only specializes in mortgages, unlike the retail lender with banking services and products like checking and savings accounts. A direct lender has more flexible guidelines and alternatives than a retail lender.
- Portfolio lender: Uses their own money to fund the borrower loan. This type of lender will set its own lending rules and is helpful for a customer who needs a large loan (a jumbo loan) or a consumer purchasing an investment property.
- Wholesale lender (a bank or other financial institution): A lender that does not work with the consumer directly, but originates, funds, and services loans. This lender will offer loans through other parties like a mortgage broker, bank, or credit union. This type of lender does not work directly with the consumer.
- Correspondent lenders: Make the loan for the consumer and can also service the loan after it closes. This type of lender will make the loan to the consumer and close. The loan is sold to an

investor, also known as a sponsor. The investor will sell the loan to Fannie Mae or Freddie Mac, a secondary market lender.

- Warehouse lender: This type of lender helps other mortgage lenders fund their loans with short-term financing. There is no contact with the consumer.
- Hard money lender: This is a private company or person that has a significant amount of cash and can fund a loan for a consumer. This is your last resort loan as they have to be repaid quickly and charge high fees and rates.
- The Mortgage Broker: A mortgage broker reviews all the rates and programs mortgage lenders offer to find you the best available deal. The mortgage broker (the person you work with) and the company they work for are called mortgage brokers. The mortgage broker does not lend you money, and the broker will not approve your loan. The mortgage broker is a licensed professional that can work with you to correct issues with your credit and finances to help you with your loan approval. The mortgage broker will collect all your documentation and provide it to the mortgage lender to get you approved for the loan. They are the intermediary between you and the lender. The lender usually pays the mortgage

broker after your loan closes, but there are instances where the broker's commission is paid directly from the borrower at closing. The draw- back to working with a mortgage broker is they do not have much control over the loan process.

Secondary Market Lenders: This is made up of Government entities: Fannie Mae, Freddie Mac, and Ginnie Mae. Many retail lenders get their money from secondary lenders. These lenders help move loan funds between states and have guidelines to help the general public. You would not go to a secondary market lender to get a mortgage.

When you decide between a mortgage lender/bank and mortgage broker, you want to weigh the pros and cons of each:

The mortgage lender/banker:

Pros:

1. Obtain a loan directly without a middle man.
2. The mortgage banker/lender can service your loan (servicing your loan means that after the loan closes, the banker/lender handles your loan payments and the management of your mortgage).

3. A banker may be able to provide special terms if you are already a customer.
4. Your loan is handled directly.

Cons:

1. Not as many loan options.
2. Limited terms.
3. You cannot shop around for different rates and terms.
4. There may not be a loan option that fits your needs.
5. A banker works for the bank, not the borrower (this is more for the retail lender).

The mortgage broker:

Pros:

1. Work with many different lenders.
2. Can shop between lenders to find you the best mortgage type.
3. The mortgage broker can help you save time finding the lowest interest rate.
4. Have more options for helping you decide what program would best meet your needs.

Cons:

1. A broker will charge a fee that may need to be paid by the borrower instead of the lender.
2. A consumer may not have a relationship with a mortgage broker as they do a mortgage banker.
3. The broker is the intermediary and does not approve the loan as the lender/banker can.

After comparing the differences, talk with several brokers and lenders to decide which would be the best fit for you.

RESEARCH YOUR LENDER

When choosing the lender you want to work with, it's essential to make sure you understand the primary loan programs being offered, such as Conventional, FHA, and VA financing.

Interview: Interview several loan officers to get an idea of who they are and how they operate. Recommendations and Reviews: Check the loan officer's reviews and ratings from other families they worked with at https://zillow. com/lender-directory this is a lender directory you can use to search reviews left by customers. You can get recommendations from the realtor. Family and friends can recommend someone they like. As a first-time home buyer, ensure you feel comfortable working with this loan officer. Trust is another essential aspect to have with your loan officer. You want them to communicate with you about what is going on throughout the process. When looking at the lender they work for, check their ratings and reviews. Make sure there is good customer service, and they are always available and approachable.

Some questions you can ask in your interview:

1. What types of loans do you offer?
2. What options are available to me based on your goals (are you concerned about the down payment, is there a specific personal situation you are worried about)
3. What is the current rate for the loan programs they discuss with you? (note rates change daily. Unless you are locked into a rate, it will change)
4. Do you offer rate locks? Is there a cost to lock my rate, and when should I lock my rate?
5. Are you going to charge any points for my rate? (A point is 1% of the loan amount). If you will pay a point or points, ask the lender to clarify how this will impact your interest rate. When you pay points, you are paying more money upfront, but you are getting a lower interest rate and paying less over time. This will be a good choice if you keep your loan for a long time.

6. How often will you contact me and what would be the best way for me to contact you?
7. Do you work with State Agencies that provide down payment assistance programs?
8. Would I qualify for a down payment assistance program if the lender works with a state agency that has them?
9. Will my loan have a prepayment penalty? (There are not many loans that have a prepayment penalty).
10. What are the costs associated with the loan?
11. What is the typical timeline to close on my loan?
12. How many families did you work with end up closing on their loans?
13. After closing, will you sell my loan?
14. What documentation will you need to start the loan process?

WHAT IS THE DIFFERENCE BETWEEN BEING PRE- QUALIFIED AND PRE-APPROVED?

They may seem like the same thing, but one is more important than the other.

Pre-Qualification: When you go house hunting, most people discuss getting pre-qualified. When you give your financial documents and asset information to the loan originator (the lender representative you are working with), you will fill out an application, and the lender reviews your information. A letter would be written to state you are qualified for a specific mortgage amount. There is no detailed review of your financial situation or history.

Pre-Approval: Some lenders offer pre-approval. You would provide the information you would need to your loan originator. Your loan originator will submit your loan into underwriting before you go out to house hunt. The underwriting department will review the loan data and issue an approval subject to finding the house and obtaining any missing items that are still needed. The company I work for has a program called Loan First. The underwriter approves the loan based on the credit with a detailed review of your financial situation. Once the underwriter issues an approval. A certificate is given to the borrower so they can provide this when they want to make an offer on the house. The certificate means the borrower went through underwriting and has full loan approval. Having this certificate/pre-approval makes you a stronger buyer to a seller because they know that you are already approved for your loan.

WHAT KIND OF INFORMATION IS ON THE LOAN APPLICATION?

The loan application is broken up into sections.

Section 1: This will include:

- Borrower information: Your name, social security number, contact information, what type of credit you are applying for (individual or joint), marital status, dependent information, and your current address. If you lived at your current residence for less than two years, you would provide your last address.
- Employment History: Information on the company you work for, the address, phone number, your position, when you started in this job, and how long you work this profession. Check if you are employed by a family member, property seller, real estate agent, or another party in the loan transaction. In this situation, additional documentation would be requested. You are self-employed if you own 25% or more of your business. Check the boxes properly for self-employment if this is the case. Then complete your gross monthly income. Lenders want to see a two-year job history. If you are working in your first job after graduating from

school and don't have a two-year job history, you can provide the information on the college or high school you attended by providing a copy of the transcripts. If there are times when you have a gap in your employment, you would want to provide the lender with a letter to explain how long you were out of work and why.

- Income: The last section would be about income from sources other than employment. This could be income from social security, a pension, disability, child support, and multiple other sources. You would need to provide your lender with documents to support the income you are receiving, like your social security award letter or disability award letter. If you are using child support to help you buy the house, you would need a copy of your divorce decree or child support agreement and proof that you received this income for the most recent six consecutive months. Income must also continue for at least three years to use it.

Section 2: Financial Data

- Assets: In this section, you will list your bank accounts, retirement accounts, and stock/mutual fund accounts.

- Liabilities: The second part would be all the debts you currently pay each month for credit cards, installment loans, or leases you may have. What kind of account it is, name of creditor, account number, unpaid balance, and your monthly payment.

Section 3: This section is for information on any properties you already own.

Section 4: This is about the loan you are applying for.

- Loan amount.
- Loan purpose.
- Purchase or refinance.
- Property address: Property address of the house you are buying, how you will be occupying the house.

-primary residence

-a second home

-investment property

-mixed-use property (will you be operating a business out of the house like a hair salon, medical office, or daycare)

- Manufactured home: A home built in a factory on a permanent chassis.
- Other Mortgages: This section asks if you have any other mortgages on the house you are buying. Some people get a second mortgage. This happens when you reach the conforming loan limit or if you are receiving a second mortgage with a government first-time home buyer program helping you with a down payment. If you buy a new house that is a 2-4 unit property, you will complete what you expect to receive in rent in this section.
- Gifts: The final area of section four is where you would list if you will be receiving any gifts or grants.

Section 5: This section asks a list of questions concerning your financial history and whether or not you are planning to live in your new home as your primary residence. It will specifically ask if you have any judgments, if you defaulted on a student loan, filed a bankruptcy in the past seven years, or had a foreclosure. If you answer yes to these questions, you will need to provide additional information to your lender about the timeframe it could affect what type of loan program will qualify.

Section 6: This section is the acknowledgment you are applying for a loan and completing it truthfully. It is where you would sign the loan application.

Section 7: This is asking about your current or prior military service.

Section 8: This section is for demographic information. The federal government wants lenders to report ethnicity, race, and sex data on the loan application.

This section exists so the government can monitor the lenders for discrimination. It was added as part of the Equal Credit Opportunity Act and the Home Mortgage Disclosure Act. It helps government regulators tell if lenders are serving the needs of their communities, identify if there are any discriminatory lending trends, and help public officials make community investment housing choices. The information is not used to make any decisions on whether or not you would be approved for the loan.

Section 9: This section is about the loan originator and their company.

WHAT DOES IT MEAN TO LOCK YOUR LOAN?

A loan lock is a promise from your lender to offer you a specific interest rate for your loan and to hold it for an agreed-upon time. When you first look for a house and check rates, you will get quotes, but rates change daily. When you lock your loan, the lender guarantees that you will close your loan with that agreed-upon rate. You can choose to pay points (1% of the loan amount) to get a lower rate. Some lenders offer a float-down option at an additional cost that you can pay so that if rates go lower after you lock your loan, you can get the benefit of lowering your rate. Loans are typically locked anywhere from 30-60 days. There are longer locks if you are buying new construction. You can pay additional money to extend your lock if necessary.

HOW DOES A LENDER CALCULATE INCOME?

Salaried Employee: If you are a salaried employee and get paid a fixed amount every pay period, the lender will look at your paystub and determine if you are paid weekly, bi-weekly or semi-monthly. For instance, if you are paid $2000 bi-weekly, $2,000 x 26 weeks/12. If weekly $2,000 x 52/12. If semi-monthly $2,000 x 24/12. The lender will review your W2 income and determine if this makes sense compared to your past earnings.

Hourly Employee: If you are paid hourly and the number of hours you work each week is guaranteed, the lender can use your hourly rate times the number of hours guaranteed for your pay each week. This would have to be verified with your pay stubs consistently showing the same hours. However, this is not the case for most hourly employees. If hours vary each week, the lender will average what you are making year to date (YTD) with your past year or two-year W2 income (this is dependent on the loan program) history.

Overtime income, bonus income, and commissions: In most instances, you would need a two-year work history to use this income. The YTD income would be averaged with what you earned for the past two years. It is up to the lender to decide if this income can be used if less than two years.

Part-time Income: You can use the income from a part-time job that you worked at the same time as your full-time job if you can show a stable history of working two jobs. The standard amount of time is two years working both jobs, but if it is typical for the type of the job you are doing, for instance, as a nurse working at multiple locations, you can use this income so long as you have been doing this for at least one year.

Self-Employed: If self-employed for more than five years, you may only need to provide one year of personal and business tax returns. This will depend on the loan program. You will most likely need to provide two years of tax returns. Your income will need to be averaged. If you have been self-employed for more than five years, you may only need to provide one year of tax returns.

There are many online sites where you can find calculators to help you see your mortgage payment for different loan amounts and how much house you can afford. hsh.com has calculators to help you with this and will even do an amortization calculator so you can see what a difference it would make to your loan term

if you made extra payments. Many major lending companies have calculators as well.

DEBT TO INCOME RATIO (DTI)

When you submit your loan application, your lender looks at your debt to income ratio. This ratio is your total monthly debt payments divided by your gross monthly income (before taxes and other deductions are taken out). This ratio determines the risk to the lender when approving your mortgage. If you wanted to do this yourself, you would need to list out all of the payments you make each month and get a total. You would not include utility bills, phone bills, or anything of that nature. Once you have that number, you would divide it by your gross monthly income.

For example, you have a car loan for $300 and two credit cards at $50 each. If the monthly debt is $400, then you would add what you think your mortgage payment would be (the payment with taxes, insurance, and any homeowner association fees) to $1500 a month. Total debt is now $1900 a month. You would divide this amount by your gross monthly income of $6500 a month. 0.29. Multiply by 100. Your debt to income ratio is 29.23%.

The ratio that your lender will accept can vary, but typically, if your DTI is less than 36%, you have a good loan which shows you can easily handle your current debt payments and the new loan payment. Lenders look closer when your DTI is between 36-43%, but it will not prevent you from getting approved. The risk becomes much greater when you get to 43-50%. You may be approved if you have other good factors like a larger down payment or a lot of money in assets. Your loan originator can work with you on your approval. You may need to pay down some debt to get your DTI lower. If you are doing an FHA or a VA loan, you may be able to go over 50% and qualify, but this means that more than half your income is going toward paying the debt. It does not allow you much room if an emergency should come up.

WHAT DOCUMENTS SHOULD I COLLECT TO GIVE MY LENDER?

- Most recent two paystubs.
- W2 and 1099 if applicable for the most recent two years.
- If you are self-employed - most recent two years' tax returns. If you have a business other than schedule C, you would need to provide two years of business returns and all K1s for all businesses.
- Most recent two months of bank statements for all of your assets. If your bank only issues statements quarterly, provide the most recent quarter. Your 401k statement is part of your assets. Make sure to send all pages.
- If you happened to own any other property, you would need the most recent mortgage statement on that house, and if the lender did not escrow for taxes and insurance, a copy of the homeowner's insurance bill, tax bill, and proof of any homeowners association bills.
- A legible copy of the front and back of your driver's license.
- If you are not a US Citizen, provide a legible copy of the front and back of your Permanent

Resident card or employment authorization card.

- If you had a divorce or have a child support agreement. The lender needs all pages of the document.
- If you receive social security or a pension, provide a copy of the award letter.
- Certificate of Eligibility for VA loan. DD214, Statement of Service or Points Statement for VA loan.
- VA Disability Awards letter for VA loan.
- If you had a bankruptcy, a copy of the discharge letter. It seems like a lot of paperwork to get together up front, but providing legible copies (not pictures from your phone) will help you fly through your mortgage loan process. If items are missing pages or are not legible, the lender will need to go back to you and ask for more information, which can slow the loan process.

STAGES OF THE LOAN PROCESS

1. Pre-qualification or Pre-Approval: Decide how you want to proceed. This is discussed earlier in this chapter. If you are in a seller's market competing against many other buyers, pre-approval would be the best way to go.

2. Completing the Loan Application: Most companies now have systems where this can be completed online.
3. Application/Processing: The loan originator may have a team of people who will work to put together all the documents provided. Lenders use different loan origination systems to check that all missing information is accounted for and documented properly.
4. Underwriting Process: The underwriter takes over once the processing of the loan is complete. The underwriter will check all the credit scores and review the information for accuracy and completeness. The underwriter ensures the loan meets all the guidelines for the loan. Many lenders use an automated underwriting system to assist in loan approval.
5. Loan Approval: When the underwriter has completed their review, loan approval or denial can be issued. If issues were found, the borrower could discuss them with their loan originator to get them resolved and receive approval.
6. Closing: After loan approval, your loan can move into the lender's closing department. The closing department will work with the title company or attorney to ensure all the numbers are correct and match. When all parties are

satisfied, the lender will send the loan documents to the title company.

WHAT ARE SOME KEY LOAN DOCUMENTS TO LOOK FOR?

You will be signing many documents as part of your loan application process. The most important would be the loan application, but you may wonder what some of the other documents are:

- The Loan Estimate (LE): When you apply for a loan, your lender is required to give you a loan estimate. This form lays out the terms of the loan you are applying for, how much you are borrowing, the estimated closing costs you will pay, and your monthly mortgage payment. This is a three-page form that gives you important details about your loan. The lender must give this to you within three business days of receiving your loan application. You can use this form to compare the information between the lenders you are interviewing. If there are any changes to your loan data, the lender will send out an updated LE form to document the change in circumstance.
- Acknowledgment of Intent to Proceed: This is a required disclosure that you are signing to

notify your lender that you want to move forward with your loan application.

- 4506-C: Lenders use this form to request your IRS tax returns or W2s.
- The Closing Disclosure: This is the final document you will see in your loan process before you go to the closing table. It is a final accounting of your loan terms. The interest rates and fees, closing costs, monthly mortgage payment, and the total of all the payments and finance charges. The lender must give you a copy of this form at least three days before you sign your final mortgage documents. You should compare this disclosure with the most recent version of the loan estimate. The required three-day time frame allows you to check all the loan details to ensure no errors in the terms or details compared to the original loan estimate you received. After you receive and sign this disclosure, if you have a change in the annual percentage rate (APR), a prepayment penalty is added (a rare occurrence these days), or the loan product switches, like changing from a fixed-rate mortgage to an adjustable-rate mortgage the lender will have to issue a new three-day Closing Disclosure.

LOAN PROGRAM OPTIONS

Conventional loans: This is a conforming loan. It complies with a set of standards from the Federal Housing Finance Agency. A conforming loan means the loan has to follow certain rules for your credit, debt, and loan size. This agency announced in November 2021, for loans purchased by Fannie Mae and Freddie Mac in 2022 that in most of the United States, "one-unit properties will be $647,200, an increase of $98,950 from $548,250 in 2021. "(*FHFA Announces Conforming Loan Limits for 2022,* 2021)

As a first-time home buyer, you may be able to qualify for a Fannie Mae Home Ready loan or a Freddie Mac Home Possible loan. These loans are suitable for a borrower that has a low income, is a first-time home buyer, and has limited funds for a down payment. Your down payment can be as low as 3%. Each program would require the buyer to complete a first-time home buyer class and provide a certificate of completion.

Non-Conforming Loans: A non-conforming loan does not fit in the guidelines for the conforming loan and is usually taken out for larger homes or for a borrower with subpar credit.

Jumbo Loan: This type of loan does not meet the limits above. They are common in higher-cost areas.

Government Insured Loan: The United States government helps to encourage homeownership by providing three government agencies that will provide backing for mortgages: The Federal Housing Administration (FHA), the United States Department of Veterans Affairs (VA loans); and the United States Department of Agriculture (USDA loans)

FHA Loans: This type of loan program helps borrowers without large down payments or excellent credit. For most lenders, borrowers will need a minimum credit score of 580 to get the maximum financing of 96.5% and have a 3.5% down payment. Some lenders will go as low as 500 credit score, but you would need to put down 10%. This type of loan requires you to pay two mortgage insurance premiums.

VA Loans: This loan program provides flexible, low-interest loans for the United States military (both active duty and veterans) and their families. You do not have to have a down payment, mortgage insurance, or a minimum credit score for this program. A VA loan charges a funding fee which is a percentage of the loan amount and can be paid upfront at closing or rolled into the cost of the loan with the other closing costs.

USDA Loans: This loan program helps moderate to low-income borrowers buy homes in rural areas. The home must be in a USDA-eligible area and qualify for specific income limits. Some USDA loans do not require a down payment. There are some extra fees, an upfront fee of 1 percent of the loan amount that you can finance in the loan and an annual fee.

Fixed-Rate Mortgage: This is where your interest rate will stay the same throughout the life of your loan. You will make the same principal and interest payment until you repay the mortgage.

Adjustable-Rate Mortgage (ARM): This is where your interest rate varies over the length of your loan. Your initial interest rate would be set below the market rate of the fixed-rate loan and will increase as the rates rise. The rate can go above the going rate for a fixed-rate loan. There are certain fixed periods where you can have your interest stay the same. You can decide on your rate being fixed from a one-month term through a ten-year term. This type of loan is more complicated than the standard fixed-rate loan. Important variables to an ARM:

- Adjustment Frequency: How often the interest rate will adjust
- Adjustment Indexes: The interest rate is based on a security standard like a treasury bill or financial index. This could be the treasury bill. Different indexes could be The secured Overnight Financing Rate (SOFR), the Cost of

Funds Index, or the London Interbank Offered Rate (LIBOR).

- Margin: When you choose to get an ARM, you would agree to pay a rate that will be a fixed percentage over the adjustment index. You would take, for example, the treasury bill rate and add two percent. The extra two percent would be the margin.
- Caps: An arm does not increase to any amount. There is a limit on how often the increases can be made. If the ARM has a cap on the mortgage payment, your loan would be considered a negative amortization loan. This keeps the payments low but only covers part of the interest. The unpaid interest is added to the principal. You could end up in a situation where your mortgage balance when the loan is paid off is greater than what you had when you took out the loan.
- Ceiling: This is the highest rate for the loan's life.(Mcwhinney, 2022)

FIXED-RATE OR ADJUSTABLE-RATE?

A fixed-rate mortgage is good if you have fixed income and do not have any tolerance for risks. You know the payment every month. The adjustable-rate mortgage (ARM) will have fluctuating rates. If your budget is flexible and you are not planning to live in the home for a long time. If you think you will earn more money in the future, a ten-year ARM would be a good option. This is a good option in the market we have today. A lower initial rate can help you get into a more expensive home.

Interest-Only Mortgages: This is a loan where you only pay the interest for a set timeframe. Once you start paying the loan's principal, the payment would increase to cover that cost. You will not be building any equity in your house while in the interest-only phase of the loan.

Piggyback Loans: This type of loan can also be called 80-10-10. It involves two separate loans. You would have your first loan for 80 percent of the home's value and a second loan for 10 percent. Then you would put 10 percent as a down payment. This can help you to avoid having to pay mortgage insurance.

Construction Loans: If you found land and want to build a home, you could decide to get a construction loan. The loan can start as a loan to cover the construction of the house and a separate loan somewhere else to pay off the loan and get a permanent loan, or you can get a loan known as a construction to permanent loan.

Balloon Mortgage: This type of loan would allow you to make payments based on a term of a 30-year mortgage but is only for a short period, like seven years. You would need to make a large payment at the end of seven years.

Individual states offer loan programs that have down payment assistance. Some have low-cost second mortgages, and some offer grants that are down payment money that would not have to be paid back. These programs can be run by the state, the county, or the city government. There are four main types of down payment assistance:

- Grants - money that does not have to be repaid.
- Second mortgage loans – loans that are paid along with your first mortgage.
- Deferred loans-this is a second mortgage that the payment would not need to be paid until you move, sell, or refinance.
- Forgivable loans - a second mortgage that is forgiven after a set number of years and would not have to be repaid unless you move, sell, or refinance too early.

Down payment assistance loan programs are usually meant for first-time home buyers, but if you have not owned a home for three years, you may still qualify for it. To qualify for this loan your primary residence must meet the purchase price limits, your first mortgage is an approved mortgage type, and you would have to work with a lender that is approved to do the loan program. Your lender should be able to tell you if they work with one of these assistance programs. You can also do a google search to find the program in your specific area.

MISTAKES TO AVOID WHEN APPLYING FOR YOUR MORTGAGE

Timing: Check your credit report before starting the mortgage process. If you find an old balance on a debt you forgot to pay off, don't pay off the debt. Major changes in your credit history can affect your credit score. If you think you might find things like this, pay off the debt six months or a year before you start applying for loans.

New Credit Cards or Installment Debt: Don't open new credit card accounts or buy a new car or furniture right before or during the time you are in the mortgage loan process.

Employment: If you are considering changing jobs, wait until after closing on the new loan. Lenders look for you to have a stable employment history.

No Lender Research: Interview loan originators with a lot of experience helping new home buyers. You want to feel comfortable working with them. You want a person that will explain everything to you each step of the way and get back to you quickly if you have any questions.

Shop: Check the rates but don't just choose the first low rate you find. You don't want to feel like you found this great rate and find out later you can only get it if you pay a lot of money.

Adding to Existing Balances: Make sure not to start charging a lot of things on your credit cards. The lender will monitor your credit through the time you close. If your monthly payments significantly increase, it could mean you may end up not being able to qualify for the loan

Save: Make sure you are putting aside money for the closing costs, moving costs, and decorating so that you are not cash-poor when you finally close.

STEP 4 : YOUR REALTOR

HOW CAN A REAL ESTATE AGENT HELP ME?

A qualified real estate agent can work with you every step of the home buying process and help prepare you for what to expect. This is especially valuable in a seller's market.

- Market Exclusives: An experienced agent has access to off-market listings, also known as market exclusives, that their office may know of but are not listed on the market for the seller's reasons.
- Experience: When you are viewing homes, your realtor will have experience and may be able to point out red flags with the property that you may not see on your own. It could help you

know that you may be looking at major repair issues or that the property's price would be much higher than it should be. Your agent knows the housing market and can give you an outside perspective on your potential home purchase.

- Tips: Most importantly, your agent can help you come up with a competitive offer. Tips to get the house when the seller has 20 other offers. Their expertise can help with creating an escalation clause. An escalation clause is a contingency in which the buyer would increase their offer to a specific dollar amount above the highest bid with a cap.
- Negotiate: When it is a slow market, your agent can help you negotiate with the seller to pay some of your closing costs.
- Solutions: Your real estate agent can help you come up with solutions if a problem arises with the house you buy at any stage of the home buying process.

You can use your real estate agent if you buy a new house from a developer. Your agent would need to be with you on your first visit to get paid a commission fee. Builders can pressure you to use all of their preferred services so that they have more control over the process.

KNOWING THE DIFFERENCE: BUYER AGENCY VS. SELLER AGENCY

A selling agent lists the property for sale. The agent works for the seller of the property that hired them. A selling agent is also known as a listing agent. Their job is to get the properties sold. It can be confusing, but the buyer's agent can also be a selling agent. This agent brings buyers to the table, which also gets the property sold.

In most instances, there is an exclusive representation between the listing agent and the seller through the listing agreement. Once there is a signed listing agreement with an exclusive right-to-sell listing, only the listing agent can get a commission for the sale of the house. The company/broker, the listing agent, works for gets the commission and shares a percentage of it with the agent.

The selling agent/listing broker cooperates with another brokerage when the other agent represents the buyer. The listing agent pays the selling brokerage part of their commission for bringing the buyer to their property.

When the listing agent is also the selling agent, the sale may be referred to as a "dual agency" The agent is a dual agent because they represent the person selling the home and the person buying the home. This term can also be applied when the company the agent works for is the same company selling the home, and the same company has another agent that brought the buyer to the home to purchase.

You can choose to hire a buyer's agent who would represent you first. If you do not have a buyer agency, your realtor would be representing the sellers of every house you view. The agent representing the seller cannot disclose anything negative that would damage the seller's position. To have a buyer's agent, you must sign a contract with an "exclusive buyer agency agreement." The buyer pays the agent a commission if the seller does not agree to pay it.

FINDING THE RIGHT REAL ESTATE AGENT

As a first-time home buyer, you want to have a real estate agent who will communicate well with you. It's a good idea to interview three prospective agents to see who would be the best fit. You can check online reviews before selecting a realtor and ask a friend or family member to give you the name of a person they thought was good.

- Your agent should be able to tell you what challenges you will run into in your local market area and help you to set realistic goals.
- Your agent should be able to help you to find homes listed at the right price for you.
- Your agent will use all their knowledge to help you create a competitive offer so you can be successful and stick within your budget.

Some questions to ask during your realtor interview:

- How many sales do you typically close in a year?

You want to make sure your realtor knows the market and understands the trends locally. There is also a difference between working with a home buyer and completing the sale by selling a home.

- Are you a full-time or part-time agent?

A full-time agent would be giving you their total focus and attention.

- Do you have a limit on the number of houses you will show me?

An agent should show you as many houses as it takes for you to find your home.

- Do you specialize in certain neighborhoods?

If there is a specific area that you want to move into, having an agent that is well acquainted with that area is important. The agent should be able to tell you about home prices, safety, schools, cultural resources, and public transportation.

- Do you charge any fees?

The seller typically pays the realtor commission.

- Will I be working with you or someone else in your office?

Many agents have a team of people that work with them. There is a benefit to working with an agent that has a team. If your agent is busy and you need to get into a property or have an unexpected issue, there would be a person on the agent's team that can handle it for you.

- How long have you been licensed?

Working with an agent with a few years of experience is better. If you want to work with a new agent, find out if there will be guidance from the broker (the person in the office that has taken educational classes beyond what the basic agent takes and manages a team of agents).

- What is your availability and schedule?

You want to ensure your agent will be available if you are in the middle of a bidding war on a property or a last-minute problem arises.

- What is the best way to contact you?

You want to understand how to best communicate with your agent. If you don't like to get texts and your agent primarily uses texts to communicate, this would not be a good fit for you.

- What percentage of your business is working with home buyers?

Most agents help both buyers and sellers, but some specialize. Having a buyer's agent would be your best option.

- How many clients do you typically work with at one time?

You want to be working with an agent who will be there for you when you need them. An agent without a team that has ten or more clients at the same time may not be able to give you the personalized service you need.

- How long does it usually take buyers you work with to find and buy a house?

It typically takes anywhere from 30 to 60 days to find a house and 14-60 days to get to the closing table.

- How will you help me find a home that matches my needs?

A good agent will give you a questionnaire to complete to help them know your home requirements. After reviewing the information, your agent will be able to let you know if what you are looking for is realistic for the area you want to live.

- Can I cancel my contract if things don't work out?

You want to ensure that if there are any issues with the agent, you will not be forced to work with them. Knowing where you stand before you start working with an agent is important.

- Do you have a list of referrals?

Every agent should have a list of referrals when they first meet with you. You need to be careful if there are no client names to give you.

- Do you have a vendor list?

An experienced agent will have relationships with other professionals like title companies, contractors, and home inspectors.

- What questions do you have for me?

You want to work with an agent interested in getting to know you and your goals with buying a house.

THINGS TO REMEMBER WHEN WORKING WITH REAL ESTATE AGENTS

- Your agent works on commission. They are highly motivated to do a good job for you so that you can close your purchase transaction.
- Be respectful of your agent's time. They have other clients, so you want to ensure you are on time for any appointments you make with them. You want to have a good partnership.
- It is better not to interview more than one agent from the same company.
- Don't contact the listing agent when working with a buyer agent. The listing agent works for the seller
- If you go to an open house without your agent, let your agent know first and give your agent's card to the listing agent hosting the open house. You would also not want to volunteer information about yourself to the open house listing agent. If you decide you like this house and want to make an offer, what you reveal about yourself could harm your negotiations.
- Make sure to discuss with your agent the best way for you to communicate with them and let your goals be known on what time frame you are working with to buy your house.

- Don't sign any forms you don't understand.
- Don't go out with the real estate agent until you are ready to buy.

WHAT IS A BUYER MARKET VS. A SELLER MARKET?

There are more homes for sale than buyers in a buyer market. This benefits the buyer because it gives them negotiating power. The seller's market is where more buyers are looking for homes than there are homes available to purchase. Sellers typically receive many offers on their house and often times, they're home selling above the asking price. Be prepared for this.

Your local real estate agent knows trends in the area you are looking to purchase in. Local real estate agents can give you their opinion on the market conditions. They can check the available inventory in the area. If local inventory is steady for less than five months' worth of housing sales, the market would be a seller's market. When there are more than seven months of inventory, it would be classified as a buyer's market. A balance of the two markets would be a balanced market with inventory sales of five to seven months that does not favor buyers or sellers. (*Determining the Local Housing Market: Buyers or Sellers Market*, n.d.)

In 2022 we are faced with a shortage of housing inventory across the country. This may lead to consider building a new house. In a seller market, the seller can get multiple offers above what they are asking. It used to be that new homes cost a lot more than resale homes, but recently that may not always be true. Building a new home also means getting a new home built with all the features you want. You don't need to worry about any renovations. You are personalizing your home. All the appliances are new and more efficient, there would be less maintenance, and many are located in planned communities that offer pools, parks, or community spaces. The drawback is that you will have to wait for it to be built, six or more months for a single-family home.

STEP 5 : THE HOUSE HUNT

LOOKING FOR YOUR DREAM HOME

Your real estate agent will start working with you to help you view open houses and keep on top of the Multiple Listing Service (MLS) to check for upcoming new properties. Your agent may also know if a house is coming on the market before it is listed on the MLS. All of your showings will be arranged by your agent. You can also sign up for new listing alerts with real estate websites like zillow.com.

YOUR HOUSE TOUR

When you go to look at prospective houses with your realtor, pay attention to

Odors: If the house you are viewing has too many candles being used and a lot of sprays and diffusers, it could be a sign of a problem. Mold and mildew odors are hard to cover up. If the person that owns the house is a smoker, it is hard to get the odor out of the walls and ceiling. It is very difficult to get rid of urine odors and stains.

Walls and Floors: You want to look at the walls and floors. Watermarks, warped floors, and large cracks in the walls could signify a major underlying problem.

Wiring and Air Flow: Make sure there is no exposed wiring and that the house has proper ventilation

Permits: Whenever you make a major change to your house, like added square footage, a garage, or a deck, you need to go to the township and get a permit. If the seller did work on the property and didn't get a permit for the new items, they are not considered legal. The town could require their removal.

When viewing the property bring a pen and paper or iPad if you prefer to your house tour so you can take notes on what you like or did not like about the house. Have a measuring tape to ensure any furniture you would want to bring with you fits in the space. It is ok to open and shut cabinets and flush the toilets in kitchens and bathrooms.

Ask your agent how long the house has been on the market and how fast they think it will sell. The agent should be able to tell you how long the current owners owned the home and why it was put on the market for sale. Keep an eye out for anything that looks like it needs repairs and if the roof appears in good condition. Write down if the home has a homeowners association as this would be an additional fee you would have to pay.

Many sellers stage their houses. Staging allows the seller to show the home in a way it would appeal to the prospective purchaser. Furniture gets rearranged to make the rooms look bigger, and you may walk into the smell of home-baked cookies to give you that homey feel. As a buyer, you need to pay attention to the floor plan and make sure it would work for the size of your family. Some stagers can remove interior doors to make rooms seem more open.

Review the seller disclosure form to see if there was a history of any major issues on the house. This disclosure form provides the buyer details about a property's condition that could harm its value. If a seller tries to hide this information from a buyer, they could be sued and even possibly convicted of a crime. Even selling the property "As Is" will not cause a seller to be exempt from this disclosure.

The following list includes common items to disclose on the seller disclosure:

- Hazards: The seller must tell the buyer if there is a concern for damage from a natural disaster or environmental contamination.
- Death: Rules vary from state to state. A seller needs to disclose if there were any deaths in the home due to violent crime.
- Nuisance from the neighborhood: This could be from a smell or noise from outside the property.
- Homeowners Association: The seller is required to disclose to the buyer if there is a homeowners association that you have to belong to and provide the financial documentation for the association.
- Repairs: Sellers need to disclose any home repairs they made on the house so the buyer can be aware of any future problem areas.
- Water Damage: If the home has flooded in the past, or anything has leaked, causing damage, the seller needs to disclose this to the buyer.
- Items in the House: A list of what will be left in the home should be on the disclosure.
- Historic Home: A seller must disclose if a home is in a historic district as it will affect how the home can be altered.

WHAT IS A COMPARATIVE MARKET ANALYSIS?

Before you make an offer on the house you like, you can ask your agent to do a comparative market analysis. A comparative market analysis estimates the home's value based on recently sold similar properties in the neighborhood. You can see the comparison of other homes that sold and are similar to the one you want to make an offer on. It will help you know that you are not making too high or too low of an offer.

BUYING A CONDOMINIUM?

What to think about if you are interested in buying a condominium. If you don't want to do any lawn work and don't want to spend time maintaining the outside of your property, a condominium might be for you. You would have to be comfortable with living in an apartment setting.

You will want to work with a real estate agent familiar with your area's condo developments. Your agent should be able to tell you if the condominium is having any financial issues or problems. Your realtor should also tell you which communities have the best resale values. Do some research on the property management company and reviews about the condominium itself.

You must check the condominium association fees, as some of them can be very expensive on top of your monthly mortgage payment. Check to see if there are or will be any special assessments.

Condominiums have different amenities. Make sure the one you are looking at has what you are looking for. Some have perks like a gym, outdoor grills, or a pool. Others just have the basic maintenance covered.

Check with your agent to make sure the condominium is FHA approved. If you need an FHA mortgage or you go to sell the unit in later years, you want to make sure there are not going to be many obstacles.

Co-op Home: A co-op is similar to a building type of a condo, but ownership is different. When you buy a co-op, you buy shares in a corporation, allowing you to live in the home. Technically it is not considered a real estate transaction. The building is jointly owned by the people living in the units, and it is considered a nonprofit corporation. The shares of ownership are based on the value of the unit. The co-op will own the interior and exterior of your unit. Anything you do to change your unit would be subject to the approval of the co-op member board. A monthly fee is paid to cover your portion of the expenses for the co-op.

OTHER HOUSING TYPES & HOW TO SEARCH FOR THEM

Fixer Uppers

A fixer-upper can help you buy a larger house in a better neighborhood. Buying a house overlooked by many potential buyers these days may be appealing. A house needing a lot of work will sell much less than one that is move-in ready. However, before looking for this kind of house, you need to know what you are getting into. Many projects are complicated, can take a long time, and are costly. They don't always go as easy as what you see on television.

If you think you can handle the renovations, different loan options can help you.

FHA 203K: This loan helps people with a lower income and credit score and can be used for most home improvement projects.

VA renovation loan: This is not a simple process. There are two loans rolled into one. The first is a home purchase loan where you would buy your house up to the current market value, and then there is a second loan. A VA home renovation loan has several key parts.

1. There is a lot of paperwork. It can take a long time because you would need to get accurate bids and have them approved.
2. There are caps on this type of loan. The amount changes between lenders.
3. The borrower cannot do any of the work themselves. A licensed contractor can only do the work.
4. Once the loan is given, the property must meet all local and state standards within 90 days (Short, 2022).

Homestyle: Guaranteed by Fannie Mae. The only requirement for the improvement is that it is permanently affixed to the property (dwelling or land). Some exceptions exist for appliances installed with a kitchen or utility room remodel. Outdoor structures like a garage, accessory unit, or swimming pool would be covered.

CHOICERenovation Loans: These loans are guaranteed by Freddie Mac. One mortgage can help you purchase the house and renovate it. You can use this loan to finance renovations that will be completed before or after it is sent to Freddie Mac. All renovations must be completed within 180 days from when the loan closes.

If you are going to take on a fixer-upper, make sure to hire a good contractor to get a solid estimate so you understand what the renovation costs may be before making an offer on the house. The type of renovation loans above requires many inspections, consults, and appraisals.

For Sale by Owner

In a market where homes are moving quickly, looking for a sale by owner house can be a good option. To find this type of listing, you can look on top online websites:

- houzeo.com
- zillow.com
- trulia.com
- FSBO.com
- forsalebyowner.com
- craigslist.com

Your real estate agent may know of any currently listed houses for sale by owner. If you use your agent to help you purchase this sale, they will want to be paid their commission. You would have to see if the house's seller would be willing to pay this.

Buying a Foreclosure Property

You can check with your county, town, or city to see if they have sites where you can see what is available.

There are several free sites where you can look up foreclosure listings:

- equator.com
- www.homepath.com
- www.homesteps.com
- Foreclosures.bankofamerica.com

There are other paid subscription sites. You can find government foreclosure listings on HUD.gov, and treasury.gov/auctions/irs. Keep in mind that the cost of the repairs on this type of property may be more than the potential savings on the house. These are proper- ties that have sat vacant for long periods. Be careful if you attend an auction for this type of property. There are bidding wars, and the houses are purchased cash only. If any debts are connected to the house, the bank that owns the property may require the debts to be paid.

Buying a Short Sale Property

A short sale is when the current owner is still living in their property and cannot make their mortgage payments. The lender agrees to let the owner sell the house for less than their mortgage debt. The lender loses money but agrees to this to avoid having to foreclose on the property. Use an experienced real estate agent when dealing with this type of property. The agent will check if a foreclosure notice was filed and how much money is owed to the lender. The bank that owns the home will be negotiating with you. This can help you prepare your offer. It can take longer to close on this type of property. When you find a property like this, you would make an offer, negotiate, provide a pre-approval letter and work with the lender to determine a sales price. Make your offer contingent on the lenders' approval of the sale and how long you are willing to wait for the approval. Have a home inspection before you buy a short sale. This type of home is sold "as-is." If the homeowner has multiple debts on the property, other lien holders could block the sale.

What to expect if a house is in probate

When a homeowner dies, the house can go into probate. This is a court-supervised legal procedure where beneficiaries legally obtain the financial and physical assets promised in a will. It can take several months to many years to get everything straightened out. The laws on what happens vary from state to state. The family would obtain the will if there were one on the property to know who would take owner- ship. Before any changes are made to the estate, a petition must be filed by the executed to the probate court. This petition would grant the legal authority to make changes. The process can take a long time. Once the family is allowed to list the house, the probate attorney would need to set a court date to finalize the sale.

Buying a new construction home

There is much more involved when buying new construction than an existing home, but in a seller's market, it may be the best option. There are three different types of newly constructed homes.

1. A custom home: The land is purchased, and you are involved in every part of the construction and planning. You would be hiring a builder and an architect who can advise you on how to move forward with the exterior and interior details of the home.
2. A semi-custom home: Usually this home would be in an area where the developer already owns the land, and you can choose between the plans of the home designs for that development.
3. Spec home or production home: The builder already owns the land, and the home is in development, but in this case, the home is already built. You can just choose a paint color and some add-ons.

Purchasing a new construction home is very similar to an existing home. A couple of things to note:

- You can still shop around for a lender, but many builders have relationships established with their lenders and title companies. You will be offered incentives to choose your preferred vendors.

- There are builder's representatives employed by the builder. It would be a good idea to have your own buyer's agent. Check to make sure the builder will pay the buyer's agent fee. If you are building a custom home, you would not need this.
- Building a new home is time-consuming. You must ensure that you have a place to live if there are delays.
- Just like you check the reputation of your lender and real estate agent, you would want to research the builder you will work with. Look for online reviews and Better Business Bureau ratings. Check with current homeowners to see how they like the neighborhoods.
- Make sure you check out the progress in a new development while checking on the builder. Check to see if people are working and if there is a lot of production. There have been instances where new buyers contract to build a home, put a substantial amount of money down between the down payment, and pay for upgrades, and then the builder goes out of business, claiming bankruptcy. If something like this happened, you would have spent all

your money and not have enough to finish your home.

- Review the rules and costs for the homeowner's association.
- You will have a lot of options for the interior and exterior items for the home. Anything you add that is not part of the standard options will be at a cost. Anytime you change, it is called a "change order."
- Hire your home inspector to ensure everything is being built as promised.

STEP 6 : THE PURCHASE

NEGOTIATING

You found the house you were looking for, and let your agent know this will be it. Now is the time to start the negotiation. Your agent will act for you.

- Act fast. The seller should respond within 24 hours. If you don't act fast, someone else can come along and get the property before you. Your agent will give you enough information to make your first offer. If you come in lower than what the seller is looking for, you may need to come up a little higher in price.

- Your agent can help you know if you should accept the counter offer or come up in price. Remember to stay within your budget.
- Increase your earnest money deposit if you want to prove you are serious to the seller.
- The seller may want a longer closing date than what you envisioned. If you think it may help the seller feel more inclined to take your offer, you can offer to let them have a later possession date and write up a rent-back agreement. A rent-back agreement is where the seller pays you rent for staying in the property for a set amount of time after the closing.
- Take out some of the contingencies in the contract. Be careful about what contingencies you remove, especially the home inspection contingency. Don't remove the loan contingency unless you can pay cash. If you remove this contingency, you agree to pay the property's purchase price even if you don't have financing.
- When you make an offer on the house, you can ask the seller to pay for some of your closing costs. It is hard to get a seller to agree to this in a seller's market, but it is something you can negotiate and remove to improve your initial bid.

- If the seller offers a home warranty that costs around $300-$600 a year, you can either remove this from the sales agreement or offer to pay for it yourself.
- Consider walking away if you are not feeling comfortable with the deal.

THE PURCHASE AGREEMENT

The purchase agreement explains the terms you agree to with the seller for purchasing the property you want. You're "under contract" once it is fully signed. This is a legal agreement that is binding.

Your realtor would typically write up and prepare the agreement using standard forms. The agreement lists the buyer and seller information, the address of the house you are buying, and the details about the house. The purchase price and any deposits are listed. If the seller is paying any of your closing costs, this would be in the agreement. The seller will make statements regarding the condition and structure of the house you buy. It will detail what kind of financing you are using to buy the house and what fixtures and appliances come with the house. It will also discuss which party is responsible for paying for the title insurance (this protects you against defects in the property). It will state the closing date and what contingencies (such as inspections or any repairs are being done) before closing. If the home were built before 1978, it would usually include a lead paint disclosure form. Each state has forms that are part of the purchase agreement.

COMMON CONTINGENCIES

This is an agreement that all parties agree to that would have to take place before the transaction can keep moving forward. Some common contingencies are

- Inspection Contingencies: Inspections benefit the buyer. It will give you a full idea of any house issues. Other inspections also fall under a general inspection, such as a pest inspection, oil tank inspection, well inspection, septic inspection, lead paint inspection, radon inspection, or mold inspection. The inspections are there to protect you.

When I purchased my first house, I did a septic inspection as part of the inspection process. It turned out that the entire septic field needed to be replaced. The cost for this was $25,000. The seller agreed to pay for the repair. If I had not done this inspection, the issue would have been found after moving in and closing. I would have had to pay for the repair. A considerable expense to cover after buying your first home.

- Financing Contingency: If you buy a home and get a mortgage, you will want a financing contingency. It gives you time to apply for your loan and receive the loan. It allows you to back out of a sale if you cannot receive financing and not lose your earnest money deposit.
- Appraisal Contingency: This is similar to the financing contingency. You can't be granted a mortgage loan if your home appraisal does not show you are purchasing a home at fair market value. If the appraisal comes in lower than the sales price, you will need to decide if you still want to move forward with the purchase and pay the difference at closing or renegotiate the purchase price with the seller. If you cannot do either of these options, you can back out of the agreement. To be more competitive in a seller's market, buyers offer an appraisal gap guarantee. This is custom wording added to a sales contract that states you will pay the difference between the appraised value and the contract price up to a specific dollar amount.
- Title Contingency: The title is a record of who owned the home from past to present and checks for liens or judgments against the property. The title company reviews this record before your loan closes to ensure your title is free and clear of issues. The title contingency

comes in if a problem comes up and you want to back out of the purchase.

DECIDING ON THE CLOSING DATE

There are several things to consider when deciding on your closing date. The seller may want a specific date, and you would not get the home if you didn't agree to it; your closing costs would be affected by the closing date; if your lock will expire and mortgage rates are rising, you would want to close before the expiration date.

Ideally, you would want to choose a closing date that is best for you and all other parties involved. Most closing dates are 30-45 days after an offer is accepted. If you close later in the month, you will pay less interest at the closing table. If you close within the first few days of the month, you will pay the interest until the end of the month, but it could give you a little more time until your first mortgage bill is due. It makes sense to want to close on a Friday so you can have the weekend to move into your house, but closing on a Friday or right before a three-day holiday weekend could lead to everyone rushing through the process. You may also want to choose a closing date based on when the moving company can get you into the house.

Communicate with your lender

As soon as all parties agree and sign the purchase agreement, you must communicate with your lender. Your real estate agent will provide your lender with a copy of the sales agreement. If you have not done so, get all the items the lender requested. This should be similar to what is listed in Step 3. If it has been a while since you gave these items to your lender, you may want to update the bank statements and the paystubs. Your lender will need a copy of your earnest money deposit check to see that it was cashed. Keep your communication channel open to ensure the lender does not need anything and check how things are progressing.

The Appraisal

When you give your sales contract to your lender, they will order an appraisal through a third-party vendor. The appraisal assures the lender that the value supports the loan amount. The appraiser determines the market value of your house by looking at comparable sales of similar houses in the same neighborhood as the house you are buying.

ITEMS TO DECIDE BEFORE YOU CLOSE

Checking on contingencies

Make sure you meet all the contingencies you have in place on your purchase agreement. If the buyer does not release the contingencies on time, the seller has the right to cancel the sale contract. The seller would give the buyer 48-72 hours to act on or release the contingency. Once the buyer releases the contingencies, the buyer has to move forward with the purchase. If the buyer does not, the seller can claim damages and keep the sales deposit money.

Owner's Title Insurance

Before your loan closes, you must let your title company or attorney know if you want the owner's title insurance. This type of title insurance is recommended but not mandatory and will protect you as the owner of your new home if a problem was found in public records or was missed during the initial title search. After closing, it may turn out there were mortgages that the prior owner did not pay off, causing an issue with the records on the property, unpaid real estate, or inheritance taxes. If you have this policy, you are protected from the cost of a legal defense and any monetary damages. It is paid for at closing and based on the home's purchase price.

The Deed

This legal document is used in a real estate transaction that transfers the property from the seller to the buyer.

It can transfer land and anything attached to the land like a house or a road. You would need a copy of your deed to prove ownership of your property. It is the record you own the property.

Title

Title is legal proof of ownership. The title and the deed are two separate things. It can be referred to as "holding title." "In property law, the title is defined by a bundle of rights that people or entities have to a particular property." (*What Does Holding Title Mean,* n.d.). These rights are a group of rights someone has to a property, including the rights of possession, control, exclusion, enjoyment, and disposition. The rights can vary depending on legal regulations and restrictions such as zoning laws, HOA rules, and other regulations. "Ultimately, the title is defined by the actual interest someone has to a property after considering all these restrictions and other legal obligations."(*What Does Holding Title Mean,* n.d.)

Your title company will want to know title vesting, which is how you want the title to your property to be held. This can vary from state to state. There are multiple ways to hold title:

Sole ownership: You are a sole owner when you own the property yourself.

Joint tenancy: When there are at least two owners, all the owners will take the title in equal percentages. If there is a death of one party, their interest would be divided by the remaining owners. No probate.

Community property with right of survivorship: Community property law does not apply to all states. If you are in a community property state and the property is owned jointly between a husband and spouse during their marriage. When one of the married partners dies, the property would automatically transfer to the surviving spouse. No probate.

Community property: In some states, this would be all property owned by a husband and wife during marriage. If there is no right of survivorship, the property must go into probate if one of the partners dies.

Tenants in common: At least two owners would be involved, and the property would be owned jointly, where each person would have the right to sell or will the property. Percentages of ownership can be equal or unequal. If one of the owners died, the property must go through probate.

TYPICAL CLOSING COSTS

Loan Origination fees are comprised of the following: Application Fee, which varies by lender.

Lenders allow you to pay money upfront to lower the interest rate over the life of the loan. Buying down the rate is called a discount point. One discount point would equal 1% of your loan amount. If you took out a loan for $100,000, you would pay $1,000 to cover the one percent discount point. These are not mandatory fees. You do have the option to buy down points in 0.125% increments.

Lenders can charge processing fees and underwriting fees.

The appraisal fee: The appraisal is ordered by the lender through a third-party appraisal management company. A professional appraiser will go to the home you are buying to evaluate how much the home is worth. The appraisal can help you ensure you are not overpaying for the property and confirm the value for the lender. Appraisal fees typically range from $300-$700, but if the house is unique, very large, or if you are asking for a rush, it could be higher.

Homeowner Association: If the house you are buying has a homeowner association (HOA), you will need to pay a transfer fee. The seller typically pays this, but if you are buying in a competitive market, you may need to cover this fee. The HOA will typically charge you the first month paid at closing. You will be provided with the payment amount and when it is due each month from the HOA.

Pest Inspections: Some states require you to get a pest inspection before you close on the loan. You can check with your real estate agent if you are in a state that requires one. A pest inspection may be recommended if the appraiser goes out to the house and notices what appears to be termite infestation or damage. A VA loan will require a pest inspection

Home Inspection: After you sign the sales contract, you will want to hire a home inspection company to go through the house to ensure there are no problems with the house you buy. There is a general home inspection. You will want to get a well or septic inspection if the property does not have public utilities. Other specialized inspections will be discussed later in the book.

Attorney Fee: You will need to pay for an attorney to close your loan if you are in a state that requires one.

Title Company: They will charge for a survey, a title search, closing protection letter, courier fee, miscellaneous transfer fees, and lenders title insurance (this is insurance to repay the bank if you lose the home due to a title claim), closing fee, and a title exam.

Credit Reporting Fee: Lenders can also charge a credit reporting fee, usually around $25.

Flood Certification: Flood Certifications are typically charged as every lender will check to see if the home you are buying is in a flood zone. The flood search fees range anywhere from $15-$25.

FHA Upfront Mortgage Insurance Premium: If you are getting an FHA loan, you will need to pay an upfront mortgage insurance premium at closing. Currently, this is 1.75% of the base loan amount.

Homeowners Insurance: This will be needed in your new home. This type of insurance protects you from liability if the home is damaged and someone gets hurt on your property. Lenders usually require that you pay the first year upfront at closing and then will collect 2-3 months at settlement to hold in an escrow account so that when the next year's payment is due, the lender will have enough funds set aside to pay it. You can shop for the best insurance rates, but it is typically $35 monthly for every $100,000 in home value. The rates will vary by state.

VA Loans: You must pay a funding fee at closing if you get a VA Loan. This funding goes toward the administrative costs for the VA loan program. The fee is based on your down payment and if you are purchasing or refinancing your house. It's also dependent on whether or not it's the first time you are using the VA loan benefit or if you used it in the past. If you are a veteran that receives disability or will apply as a surviving spouse of a veteran who died in service or as a result of a service-related disability, you are exempt from the funding fee. If you get a first-time VA loan and put down less than 5%, the VA funding fee would equal 2.3% of the total loan value. If it's not used for the first time, it would be 3.6%. If you put down 5%, the fee would be lowered to 1.65%, and 10% would lower your fee to 1.4%. Whether it's your first or fifth time utilizing the VA loan, this fee would not change. The fee is different if you are refinancing a VA loan into another VA loan.

Owner's title insurance: This is optional. Title insurance will cover you if there is a title issue. You will be covered if a previous owner were to bring a lawsuit against you after you close on your purchase of the property. For example, if a lien is found on the title five years after you buy your house, the title insurance company would need to reimburse you the coverage on your policy.

Taxes and other government fees: You typically pay a recording fee to the local city or county government for them to update the public land ownership record. You will also be charged transfer taxes paid to your local government to show the property is now transferred to you. The fees vary depending on where you live.

Pre-Paid Fees: These fees include:

Homeowners insurance and Mortgage Interest. The homeowner's insurance 12-month premium discussed earlier, mortgage interest(this is the interest that accrues on your loan from the date of your closing to the date of your first mortgage payment. The amount varies based on your interest rate and closing date): (Local government charges a fee for the public services in the area, like schools, roads, and fire departments).

The amount you pay will depend on the home value and the location of your house. A lender can require you to pay up to a year at closing. Mortgage interest to the end of the month: This will be charged at closing and includes your closing date to the end of the month. If you close at the beginning of the month, the amount would be higher than if you closed at the end of the month.

Private Mortgage Insurance: Private mortgage insurance is charged on a conventional loan if you put less than 20% of the sales price down on your home. This protects the lender if you default on the loan. It would also be part of the prepaid fees. You will pay the first month's premium at closing. It can range from $30-$70 each month for every $100,000 borrowed. You also have an option to pay for part or all of the private mortgage insurance (PMI) upfront at closing to eliminate your paying it monthly in your monthly mortgage payment. On a conventional loan you can contact your lender once your loan to value is 80% or less to have the PMI removed. An FHA loan also has an upfront insurance premium paid in addition to a monthly mortgage insurance premium (MIP) fee for the life of the loan unless you have a down payment of 10% or more. The MIP can come off after 11 years if you have a larger down payment. If you get a USDA loan, there is an upfront and an annual guarantee fee.

Administration Fee: Realtors can charge an administration fee.

Locking your rate: If you lock your interest rate with a lender, you can also be charged a fee to lock your interest rate.

Reserves: Having reserves means you have enough money in the bank after the closing to cover your full mortgage payment for typically two months. Some lenders will require that you have this in your assets before closing. The number of months of reserves will vary based on the loan program you qualify for and your credit score.

PLANNING YOUR MOVE

There are many things to remember during a move. Prepare a checklist, so you don't miss something important. Contact all the utility companies to schedule to shut off your utilities in your existing residence and turn on your service in the new location, get your mail forwarded, and get all your packing materials.

Moving is expensive. Do you want to make a full-service move where the moving company comes in and packs all of your belongings and moves them, or will you do it yourself? Get some estimates from moving companies or contact companies that you can rent the truck and buy all the boxes and packing material.

Hiring a Mover

When you have so much going on, taking the time to pack up your things can add to your stress. You can save time and energy and hire a professional moving company. Like all the other professionals you worked with on your purchase, you want to hire an experienced moving company. This company needs to be licensed and in the business for some time. You trust your possessions with this company, so you want to do your research. The professional moving company can do other duties besides moving boxes:

- Supply moving supplies such as bubble wrap and boxes.
- Offer packing services.
- Take apart and assemble your furniture for you.
- Know how to move your fragile items or priceless art pieces.
- Expertise in moving a piano.

When you contact the builder, they will need to come out and see what items you are moving to give you an estimate on the cost. You can then check with the company about the other services they offer. They will be able to tell you if they are charging an hourly or flat rate and if they can move any specialized furniture you may have. You may need to pay a deposit to secure your moving date.

If you decide to hire a moving company, there are a few things your movers would want you to know:

- Don’t get in the mover's way while doing their job. They know you want to be helpful, but you hired them as professionals.
- If the movers are not packing for you, ensure you are done with all the packing the day before.

- Keep your cash, jewelry, and prescription medications with you. Movers don't want to be worried about this type of valuable.
- Label your box with Fragile if you have breakable items in it.
- Check the area to be sure the movers have a place they can park their truck and the best way to access your place.
- Stay close enough to the movers if they need you but not in their way.
- It is standard practice to tip your movers. Usually $25-$50 per mover or 10% to 15% for the total cost of the move. (*Moving Day Etiquette: 10 Things Movers Want You to Know*, n.d.)

Before the move, sort through your things and try to declutter. Purge all items you no longer use or need. By purging items, you no longer use, you save yourself from moving useless items and the extra cost of moving them. Pack your essential items separately: important documents, medications; chargers; change of clothing, and basic toiletry items. Stock up on packing supplies, paper towels, and garbage bags. Have more boxes than what you think you need, so you do not have to worry if you fall short at the last minute. It is essential to rent a truck that has a ramp. It is more money but tiring lifting heavy furniture and boxes without a ramp.

- Use the right size box for the correct items. Put the heavy items in small boxes and light items like pillows and linens in large boxes.
- Put the heavy items on the bottom and the lighter items on the top, and when you are loading the boxes, pack the heavier boxes near the front of the truck to help with balance.
- Fill in all empty spaces in the boxes. You can put clothing or packing paper to fill in the gaps.
- Pack all items from the same room in each box. Don't mix different rooms in one box.
- Label your boxes. This lets the mover know where to take the box once arriving at your destination. You can also put different color stickers on your boxes to facilitate the organization between rooms.
- Use a good amount of tape to ensure the boxes are secure.
- If you need to move an expensive art item, check with the company you are getting your boxes and truck from and see if you can purchase specialized crating.
- Pack your kitchen correctly. Don't pack your dishes so that they are flat. Make sure to put packing paper around every dish and then wrap

them in bundles. Pad the items well with bunched-up paper. There are dish-barrel boxes you can use to pack these items. You can purchase cardboard dividers to help protect your glasses.

- You can leave your clothes in your dresser and wrap them with plastic to prevent the drawers from falling out. Just make sure the dresser is not too heavy for you to move if you do this. There are wardrobe boxes you can purchase to put all the hanging clothes. When packing your shoes, you want to wrap each shoe separately and put socks in each shoe to hold their shape.
- Put your television in a box, and then put that box inside another box that has padding.
- If you are taking apart something with a lot of wiring, take a picture with your phone, so you know how to put it back together. Having the picture will help you if something valuable gets broken. You would be able to claim it on your insurance.

THE HOME INSPECTION

What is a home inspection, and when should it be done?

This is a visual inspection of a house's structure and its systems from the foundation to the roof. This type of inspection can take from two to four hours, but it all depends on the size of the home you are buying. The home buyer will usually get a report copy within 48 hours. This copy will have photos and will let you know what items are functioning correctly or what needs to be repaired. According to Angie Hicks, co-founder of the home services website Angie's List, home inspections are dependent on location and the size and age of the home. You should expect a cost of approximately $300-$450 (Lee, 2019).

The standard home inspector's report will cover the condition of the home's:

- Heating system.
- Central air conditioning system (temperature permitting).
- Interior plumbing system.
- Electrical system.
- The roof.
- Attic.
- Visible insulation.
- Walls.
- Ceilings.
- Floors
- Windows and doors

- The foundation
- Basement
- Structural components

You can find a more detailed outline covered in the home inspection report here:

homeinspector.org. ASHI Standard of Practice and Code of Ethics.

A home inspection protects you from unexpected problems with your future home. It can also help you learn how to maintain systems in the new home.

You don't have to be at the home inspection, but it is valuable to gain upfront knowledge and ask questions while you are there. If your inspection reveals a problem, you can go back to the seller and negotiate what repair items would be taken care of to move forward. There are cases where you, as the buyer, may decide you do not want to move forward with the purchase after the home inspection.

The following is a list of other specialized home inspections you may want to do:

- Roof Inspection (only if your general home inspector found an issue)
- Chimney Inspection (only if your general home inspector found an issue)

- Lead Paint Inspection for homes built before 1978
- Pest, termite, or rodent inspection
- Radon Gas Inspection (your general home inspector may be able to do this)
- Asbestos Inspection
- Mold Inspection
- Septic System Inspection
- Well water inspection
- If your general home inspection found items that may be structural, you would want to get a foundation or structural inspection
- Underground oil tank inspection.

Your main concern in getting a home inspection completed on the home you are looking to purchase is to make sure you will uncover any major repairs before removing your inspection contingency. The following is a list of the ten most expensive home repairs:

1. Foundation-A foundation repair can cost anywhere from $450-$11,000.
2. Roof replacement-The average cost to repair or replace a roof can run anywhere from $650-$6,000.
3. Hot water heater-A repair can run $523 whereas a replacement can be $1000

4. Termite damage-Treating for termites can be about $541, but fixing damage can be around $7,229.
5. Water damage-Average repair cost is $2,330.
6. Plumbing-A sewer line repair can average $2,443, a drain pipe $559, and new pipes $1,054.
7. Heating/Air Conditioning: A repair can cost around $372 for an air conditioning unit and $288 for a furnace.
8. Mold removal: Average cost is $2,155
9. Electrical problems: The average for repair is $318, but if the entire house needs to be rewired, it could average $15,000
10. Septic repair: This can average $1,488 (Zebra, 2021).

Inspections and new home construction: Don't overlook your final walk-through even if everything is new. Doing a whole home inspection is still a good investment before you close. Because this is a new home, you will be the first person to test out all the systems. A home inspector can test all the systems, show you how they operate and confirm they are working correctly. There could be code issues that were missed. If you wanted to be thorough, you could hire a home inspector to look at the house before the walls are closed in and after the home is completed.

HOMEOWNER INSURANCE AND HOME WARRANTIES

Protection for your Home

Homeowner's insurance is essential. Your lender for the house you are going to purchase will require that you have homeowners insurance. It protects your home from damage and protects you from personal liability for any damage or injuries that may happen in your house or on your property. It is like a security blanket for your home.

If your house is in an area that frequently floods, you will need flood insurance.

Once you have a fully signed sales contract, you should start shopping around for a company to provide you with homeowners insurance. There are many companies where you can go online and put in basic information that will compare what different companies offer. usnews.com/insurance/homeowners-insurance has a chart on their site and gives you a list of insurance companies that they consider are best, along with some detail about each company. Once you have the company you want to use, contact your loan originator or assistant and let them know the company's name, who you are working with, and the phone number. Give the loan originator a copy of a quote or a reference number. The lender will need to provide your homeowner's insurance company information to put on the policy as the lender will be listed as your lien holder. The lender will need a copy of the policy and an invoice to be paid at the closing.

A different insurance policy is needed if you are buying a condominium. This policy type is an HO-6 condo insurance policy. This policy covers structural improvements inside your condominium, your personal belongings, personal liability, and any losses your condominium association makes you pay. When you purchase a condominium, the association has a master insurance policy. This would cover everything outside of your condominium unit. In most cases, you would be responsible for everything inside your unit. Your mortgage company will want you to have building coverage equal to 20% of the appraised value to protect their interests.

WHAT KIND OF PROTECTION IS IN A HOMEOWNERS INSURANCE POLICY?

- Dwelling Protection-this is one of the policy's basic coverages for the structure of the home and any structures attached to the home like a garage or a deck. If you have other structures on your property like a shed, fence, or detached garage, you would need to have this coverage added separately. In 2022, on average in the United States, homeowners insurance cost is an average of $1383 per year for a dwelling policy with coverage of $250,000 (Decenter, 2022).

- Personal Property Protection-Your policy will protect your personal belongings in your home. If someone came in and stole your electronics or anything valuable in your house or your house was damaged by fire. You can get money to replace them. You can purchase extended coverage to protect items like jewelry and watches that may have value over the basic personal coverage limits.
- Liability Protection-Liability inspection is to protect you if someone who does not live with you is injured while they are on your property. You would be covered for any legal expenses and medical bills. You should have enough liability insurance to protect your assets. A minimum of $100,000 of liability insurance is common with most homeowner insurance policies. The recommended liability insurance is purchasing at least $300,000 to $500,000 coverage. (*How Much Homeowners Insurance Do I Need*, n.d.)

- Loss of Use-This will help you pay temporary living expenses while your home is being repaired.

Just like with car insurance, there are coverage limits and deductibles. Your homeowner's insurance will cover your house for fire, wind, and snow but does not cover floods or earthquakes. Besides adding additional endorsements for jewelry, there are some other added items to think about.

- Ordinance or law coverage - this coverage would bring your home up to current codes during any repairs or rebuilding
- Water backup coverage-this pays for damage from backed-up sewer lines, drains, or sump pumps. I had my sump pump fail and was not aware this coverage when my basement flooded and it was not covered in my policy, so I had to pay the cost myself. I learned the hard way. Make sure to add this additional coverage if you have a sump pump.
- Equipment breakdown coverage-this will pay for HVAC systems and large appliances if they stop working for reasons other than wear and tear.

- Service line protection- Covers damage to water, electric, or other utility lines that are your responsibility.
- Identity fraud coverage-this would pay for expenses like lost wages or legal fees due to identity theft.

If you have a claim on your insurance policy, you would need to contact them and file a claim. Your payout would vary based on what kind of coverage and deductible options you have.

INSURANCE COVERAGE

There is three basic levels of coverage.

- Actual cash value: This would cover the cost of your house and the personal items after depreciation is deducted
- Replacement Cost: This covers the actual cash value of your house and personal items without considering depreciation
- Guaranteed replacement cost: This offers the most coverage. It has enough coverage to repair or replace your house, even if it is more than the policy limit.

INSURANCE DEDUCTIBLE

The deductible is the amount you would have to pay before the insurance company covers any of your claims. The higher your deductible, the lower the rate; the lower the deductible, the higher the rate. There are two types of deductibles: flat dollar amount or percentage amount.

1. Flat dollar amount deductibles- This is the standard, fixed-dollar amount deductible you pay out of pocket when you file a claim for a covered property damage loss. "A standard homeowners insurance policy deductible is usually $500 to $2,000, although lower and higher deductible home insurance plans are also common." (Howard And McGinley, 2022)
2. Percentage deductibles-Percentage deductibles are specific to wind/hail, named storms, and hurricane- related claims. They're calculated based on the percentage — usually 1% to 10% — of your home's insured value (i.e., the dwelling coverage limit in your policy). These deductibles typically only apply if you live in an area at high risk for hurricane or wind damage. If your house is insured for $200,000, for instance, and your policy has a 1% hurricane

deductible, $2,000 would be deducted from the claim payment" (Howard And McGinley, 2022).

THE HOME WARRANTY

A home warranty is a protection to help cover the cost of service, repair, or replace major appliances and systems. It is often offered in the purchase agreement for older homes. Any party in the transaction can purchase the warranty. If the seller offers the warranty, it would be a more specific, limited warranty that will offer financial protection to the buyer if something goes wrong with a major system. There is no coverage to repair less expensive appliances. If the housing market is a buyer market, it is a good incentive for the seller to offer this to the buyer. When it is a buyers market, the buyer would most likely pay for a home warranty- if one is wanted. The warranty purchased by the buyer usually covers both large and small appliances and major home systems the buyer chooses. The typical cost of a one-year home warranty generally costs around $300 to $600. Approximately $20,000 worth of systems and appliances are generally covered in this price range. (Reynolds, 2021)

Home Warranty on New Construction

When you hire a builder, they will give you a builder warranty. This covers items that are a permanent part of the home, like your electrical work, plumbing, and concrete floors. The builder warranty offers limited coverage for quality and materials. Typically a year coverage for workmanship and materials; two-year coverage for HVAC, plumbing, and electrical; ten years coverage for major structural defects.

STEP 7 : CLOSING

THE FINAL WALK THROUGH

The final walk-through is a physical tour of your new house right before the closing. It is important to do this walk-through because you are making sure that the house you are buying is left in the condition you agreed upon when you purchased it. You would attend the final walk-through with your real estate agent and the house would typically be empty. If your purchase contract states the house should be left in "broom swept" condition, the entire house would be empty, the carpets vacuumed, countertops cleaned, floor swept, and no personal debris from the prior owner.

The following is a list of items to check when you do your final walk-through:

- Check heating and air conditioning (weather permitting).
- Check electrical-both the outlets and the lights.
  Look in the kitchen and ensure all the shelves and the doors are in good shape.
- Check all appliances work.
- Look around to ensure there are no insects in the house.
- Check that all the landscaping is intact (no major shrubs, trees, or plants are missing).
  Check the bathrooms so that everything flushes and runs properly.
- Check that all the windows can open and shut and if any of the screens are missing.
- If you have an attic or basement, check that there are no signs of recent leaks.

WHAT HAPPENS AT THE CLOSING TABLE?

You finally reached the finish line! You are now the owner of your new house. You are going to be signing anywhere from 50-100 pages of documents. Make sure you are asking questions and read everything you are signing. By now, you would have already received your final closing disclosure with the closing costs and know what money you should bring to closing. To ensure everything goes as planned, bring your photo ID, any outstanding papers that your loan originator or title company asked you to bring, and a certified check made payable to the title or closing company for closing costs. You also can get the title company's wiring instructions and wire the funds.

One important note on wiring funds. There are a lot of scammers out there. If you receive wiring instructions from your title company via email or text, you need to double-check the information with the title company directly over the phone. There are scammers stealing title company and mortgage company emails and posing as a trusted party in the purchase transaction to get you to wire the funds to the wrong place. Getting your money back if you are tricked into doing something like this would be next to impossible. Wire fraud issues are email hacks. The hackers get into the email accounts of the closing agent, attorney, or real estate broker and monitor what is being discussed. They wait for the right time and copy the owner of the account's email to send the fraudulent wire instructions to the home buyer, who is unaware of anything going on. They ask the buyer to send the funds to the hacker's email account and give information to call a number to confirm the wire. The hacker could also hack you as the buyer and follow your emails to get information. Keep in mind:

1. Never wire funds to anyone unless you have double-checked separately with the title company or settlement agent that it is correct.
2. If you can't get a hold of someone at the title company, check to see if their wiring instructions are posted online.
3. Some agents will confirm the instructions by phone, and you need to confirm you are speaking to the correct person. Call them back on a publicly listed phone number and ask for the correct person.

You will sign all the legal documents and pay your closing costs and escrow items at the closing. A few key items you will be signing are:

- The Loan estimate-This form has important information on your loan. Double-check all the information is correct.
- Promissory note or "Note" - This is the agreement of the terms of the mortgage you are taking out and is your promise to repay the mortgage.
- Mortgage or deed of trust- this document secures the note and gives your lender a claim

against the home if you don't meet the terms of the mortgage note

- Initial escrow statement - this form will tell you what the lender will be paying from your escrow account for the first year of your mortgage for taxes and insurance
- Closing Disclosure -This is similar to the loan estimate and outlines everything in your mortgage. You would have received a copy of this three days before closing.
- Monthly payment letter - The lender will give you a letter outlining your payment and where you would send your first payment.

All the parties in the real estate transaction do not need to be at the closing on the same date and time. You will be meeting the closing agent, attorney, or title company representative. Other parties involved in the sale, such as the seller's real estate agent, your agent, and your loan originator, might be there.

Once everything is signed, you can breathe a sigh of relief and start the celebration. The house is yours! You will get your keys. Keep a copy of all the mortgage paperwork in a safe place.

MOVING IN

If you have the time and a place to stay, consider a few projects for your new home before unpacking all your boxes and settling in.

1. Paint the rooms. Now is the time to put your personal touch on your new house. Once you move everything in, it's much harder to have your furniture and belongings in the way.
2. If you are planning to make any changes to the flooring, install new floors before everything is set in its place.
3. If you are planning any significant updates to the electric or plumbing, this would also be a good time to do them. Especially if you are planning to remodel a kitchen or bathroom

HOME MAINTENANCE

Now that you are a homeowner, home maintenance should be considered. If a breakdown or something in the house needs to be replaced, you will need to take care of it. Start early and put home maintenance in the budget. The rule of thumb is to set aside 1% of the home's purchase price for repairs and replacement costs. If you purchased an older home, you might want to set aside a little more than that figure. A home maintenance schedule is essential. Maintenance Items to check:

- Clean/replace the furnace filter to remove dust build-up. This should be done every three to six months.
- Check for mineral deposits in faucets and shower heads
- Test all smoke alarms, fire extinguishers, ground fault interrupters, and carbon monoxide detectors to ensure they are still working
- Clean your garbage disposal by grinding ice cubes and washing it out with hot water and baking soda.
- Check your gutter to make sure they are free of leaves and downspouts are connected properly
- Maintain any shrubs to make sure they are not too close to your house.
- In the spring, power wash the house siding and windows
- Have your heating/air conditioning system checked twice a year
- Check to seal any cracks or gaps in the windows and doors
- Check your driveway and seal any cracks or gaps

- Before winter, drain and winterize any exterior plumbing.
- Hire a professional to check your fireplace before using it in the fall.

Document Protection: Make copies of your closing documents and store them in a safe place. You can opt to copy them and store them in a secure cloud-based site, google drive, or dropbox.

- Safety First: Change the locks or rekey the locks. This is important for your safety as you have no idea if all of the keys are accounted for when you are given them at the closing table.
- Many newer homes have keypads. Make sure to update the codes.
- Make sure everyone knows you moved. Besides your friends and family, your bank must have your new address. Change your address on your driver's license. All credit card companies and installment debt companies would need your new information.
- Check you have enough hot water Deep clean the house
- Go out and meet the neighbors. This is a great time to exchange contact information if there is an emergency and learn some positive things about your new community.

AFTERWORD

I hope you enjoyed reading this book. My hope is that you can refer back to the various sections as you go through the home buying process. I hope the information in this book will make it less intimidating and help you feel more confident in your home purchase. Now that you have all the tools, it's time to go out and use them. Best of luck in finding your dream home!

If you enjoyed this book, kindly leave a review on Amazon.

BUYING YOUR FIRST HOME
SCAN ME

GLOSSARY

401K: An employment-sponsored retirement plan. The employee can contribute money from each paycheck before taxes are deducted. Each company has different investment options. Taxes are not required to be paid for a withdrawal if you take the money after age 59.5. Some companies will match the funds you contribute up to a specific amount. Some companies allow you to borrow funds from the money you save and pay your- self back over time.

Abstract of Title: It is a history of the parcel of land. The history is checked to make sure there are no claims on the property.

Adjustable-Rate Mortgage (ARM): A loan where the rate of the mortgage adjusts over time. An ARM would generally start with a lower rate that changes over time.

Amortization: When you take out a mortgage, the payments are amortized. This is a payment schedule that will show how much the borrower will pay toward interest and principal over the life of the loan.

Annual Percentage Rate (APR): The interest rate on your loan that includes the interest plus all of the other fees you will pay during the entire loan process. It is the calculation of how much money you are paying to borrow the money.

Appraisal: An unbiased professional opinion of the value of a home. It will tell a lender what a house is worth.

Appreciation: An increase in the value of property or goods.

Assumable Mortgage: An arrangement where an outstanding mortgage and its terms are transferred from the current owner to the buyer. The buyer has to qualify to assume the mortgage but would not have to get their own mortgage. This option is available on a USDA, FHA, and VA loan.

Bankruptcy: A person or business that cannot pay its debts can engage in a legal transaction where the court will decide if the debts will need to be repaid.

Closing Disclosure (CD): The final document given to a borrower by their lender that lists the details of the loan transaction. The borrower is given three days to look at the information and sign it.

Collection Account: Unpaid bills that are typically from utility companies, rent, or medical procedures.

Credit Tradeline: Each credit account you have is listed on your credit report. There are installment tradelines like a student loan, car loan, or mortgage and revolving credit lines like your credit cards. Each credit debt is called a tradeline.

Curb Appeal: The general appeal of a house or property from the outside to a buyer.

Debt Ratio: The ratio of the total amount of debt compared to the total assets.

Deed: A legal document that transfers ownership of an asset from the current owner to the new owner.

Deed of Trust: A document also known as a trust deed is used in real estate transactions. It transfers the legal title of a property to a lender until the borrower repays the debt in full.

Earnest Money Deposit (EMD): A buyer gives the seller money in good faith when they offer to buy a home.

Equity: The value of a property after deducting the amount of money owed on it.

Escrow: Assets held by a third party in a real estate transaction.

Fair Credit Reporting Act (FCRA): A federal law that requires companies to be fair and accurate and to ensure consumer privacy.

Fair Isaac Corporation (FICO): The credit score that shows on credit reports and is used by lenders to access credit risk.

Federal Home Loan Mortgage Corporation (FHLMC or Freddie Mac): A government-sponsored agency that purchases mortgages from lenders. It was created to provide more liquidity and stability in the housing market.

Federal Housing Administration (FHA): An FHA loan is a loan backed by the U.S. government.

Federal National Mortgage Association (FNMA or Fannie Mae): A government-sponsored agency that purchases mortgages from lenders. The mortgages are sold as securities to keep housing affordable.

Foreclosure: The legal process where a lender will take ownership of a mortgaged property when the owner missed a specific number of payments in order to recover the amount owed on the loan.

Government National Mortgage Association (GNMA or Ginnie Mae): A government agency that guarantees timely payments of Mortgage-Backed Securities. It exists to provide liquidity in the home loan market.

Home Equity Line of Credit (HELOC): a line of credit that is given to a borrower that can be accessed as needed using the equity in a home for collateral.

Home Owner's Association (HOA): A community of homes that is governed by an association. The HOA is typically in a planned community and manages the neighborhood. There are usually rules that are enforced by the association to cover how common areas are maintained.

Housing Bubble: Housing prices are increasing quickly due to a rise in demand, causing the market to collapse. This usually happens when there is more demand for housing than supply.

Itemize: When you itemize on your tax return, you are listing allowable tax deductions.

Judgment: A court decision that determines what each party in a dispute is is legally responsible. Typically the dispute is over money. The court decision is legally binding.

Lien: A legal claim against a property that is recorded with the local government that gives the lienholder the legal right to be paid when the property is sold. If you were to sell a property, the lien would need to be satisfied before the property could transfer to a new owner.

Loan Estimate (LE): A three-page document that lists the loan information in a standardized manner. It allows the consumer to compare the costs between different lenders. The LE must be given to a borrower within three business days of applying for a mortgage.

Loan Lock: A lender will offer a borrower a rate for a loan. When you lock your loan, the lender is holding the agreed-upon rate for a specific period of time.

Mortgage: A loan used to purchase a home.

Probate: When a person who owns a home dies, their belongings have to go through a court process called probate. The court will carry out the details listed in a will or follow the state law if there is no will on how to manage the property. The court would need to approve the sale of the real estate if there is no will or the will does not state how the handle the real estate.

Short Sale: A sale of a property where the lender agrees to let the owner of the property sell it for less than what is owed on the mortgage. The lender would do this instead of taking the home from the homeowner for not making payments.

Title Insurance: A form of insurance that protects the owner against problems with the title to the property. The lender will require a borrower to obtain the lender's title insurance. The buyer has the option to obtain the owner's title insurance.

US Department of Agriculture Loan (USDA Loan): A government-backed loan that does not require a down payment for buyers purchasing homes in rural areas.

Veterans Administration Loan (VA Loan): A loan backed by the US government created to assist veterans, service members, and their surviving spouses purchase a home with little to no downpayment.

Zoning: Cities or towns designate specific areas to have a certain type of building and how the buildings are used.

BIBLIOGRAPHY

2022 Cost of Living Calculator. (n.d.). Bestplaces.Net. https://www.bestplaces.net/cost-of-living/

D'Angelo. (2021, November 14). *Do credit repair companies really work.* Https://Www.Investopedia.Com/Do-Credit-Repair-Companies-Really-Work-5076928.https://www.investopedia.com/do-credit-repair-companies-really-work-5076928

Determining the Local Housing Market: Buyers or Sellers Market. (n.d.). Https://Www.Zillow.Com/Sellers-Guide/Buyers-or-Sellers- Market/. https://www.zillow.com/sellers-guide/buyers-or-sellers- market/

Deventer. (2022, June 9). *Average cost of homeowners insurance in june 2022.* Https://Www.Bankrate.Com/Insurance/Homeowners-Insurance/Homeowners-Insurance-Cost/. https://www.bankrate.com/insurance/homeowners-insurance/homeowners-insurance-cost/

FAQsabouthomeinspection.(n.d.).Https://Www.Homeinspector.Org/Buyers-And-Owners/Homebuyers-Guide/FAQs-about-Home-Inspection.https://www.homeinspector.org/Buyers-And-Owners/Homebuyers-Guide/FAQs-about-Home-Inspection

Dictionary. (n.d.). Https://Www.Investopedia.Com/Financial-Term-Dictionary-4769738. Retrieved July 2, 2022, from https://www.investopedia.com/financial-term-dictionary-4769738

Find the Best Places to Live. (n.d.). Find The Best Places To Live. https://www.areavibes.com/

FHFA Announces Conforming Loan Limits for 2022. (2021, November 30). Https://Www.Fhfa.Gov/Media/PublicAffairs/Pages/FHFA-

Announces-Conforming-Loan-Limits-for-2022.Aspx.https://www.fhfa.gov/Media/PublicAffairs/Pages/FHFA-Announces-Conforming-Loan-Limits-for-2022.aspx

Homebuyers should never skip the final walk through here's why. (2021, July 6). Https://Houwzer.Com/Blog/Home-Buyers-Should-Never-Skip-the-Final-Walk-Through. https://houwzer.com/blog/home-buyers-should-never-skip-the-final-walk-through

Howard And McGinley. (2022, April 4). *Homeowners insurance deductible explained.*Https://Www.Policygenius.Com/Homeowners-Insurance/What-Is-a-Homeowners-Insurance-Deductible/.https://www.policygenius.com/homeowners-insurance/what-is-a-home owners-insurance-deductible/

How much homeowners insurance do i need. (n.d.). Https://Www.Ii-i.Org/Article/How-Much-Homeowners-Insurance-Do-You-Need#:~:text=Most%20homeowners%20insurance%20policies%20provide%20a%20minimum%20of%20%24100%2C000%20-worth,%24500%2C000%20worth%20of%20liability%20coverage. https://www.iii.org/article/how-much-homeowners-insurance-
do-you-need#:~:text=Most%20homeowners%20insurance%20poli cies%20provide%20a%20minimum%20of%20%24100%2C000% 20worth,%24500%2C000%20worth%20of%20liability%20coverage.

Investopedia Team. (2021, March 11). *Credit Score.* Https://Www.Investopedia.Com/Terms/c/Credit_score.Asp. https://www.investo pedia.com/terms/c/credit_score.asp

Kearns. (2022, June 12). *What are the main types of mortgage lenders?*
Https://Www.Investopedia.Com/Mortgage/Mortgage- Guide/Mortgage-Lenders/.RetrievedJune26,2022,from
https://www.investopedia.com/mortgage/mortgage-guide/mortgage-lenders/

Kinney, Brown, Lobb. (2022, May 31). *Best Homeowners Insurance Companies of 2022.* Https://Www.Usnews.Com/Insurance/Homeowners-Insurance. https://usnews.com/insurance/homeowners-insurance

Laney. (2022, April 13). *Knowing the difference between a mortgage banker and a mortgage broker can help you get the most for your money.* Https://Www.Businessinsider.Com/Personal-Finance/Mortgage-Banker-vs-Mortgage-Broker. Retrieved June 26, 2022, from https://www.businessinsider.com/personal-finance/mortgage-banker-vs-mortgage-broker

LaPonsie. (2022, April 28). *Understanding Housing Inventory and What It Means for you.* Https://Realestate.Usnews.Com/Real-Estate/Articles/Understanding-Housing-Inventory-and-What-It-Means-for-You#:~:text=As%20of%20mid%2DApril%202022,level%20ever%20recorded%20last%20December.https://realestate.usnews.-com/real-estate/articles/understanding-housing-inventory-and-what-it-means-for-
you#:~:text=As%20of%20mid%2DApril%202022,lev

Lee. (2019, July 15). *How much does a home inspection cost?*
Https://Www.Bankrate.Com/Real-Estate/How-Much-Does- Home-Inspection-Cost/.https://www.bankrate.com/real-estate/ how-much-does-home-inspection-cost/

Leonhardt. (2019, July 23). *How to turn your place into an unforgettable (and potentially lucrative) Airbnb rental.* Https://Www.Cnbc.-Com/2019/07/23/How-to-Turn-Your-Place-into-an-Airbnb-Rental.Html.https://www.cnbc.com/2019/07/23/how-to-turn-your-place-into-an-airbnb-rental.html
el%20ever%20recorded%20last%20December.

Marino & Gomez. (2019, August 29). Top Improvements that increase home value based on market data. Https://Www.Opendoor.Com/w/Blog/Improvements-That-Increase-Home-Value#:~:text=Should%20I%20add%20another%20bathroom,shower%2C%20sink%2C%20and%20toilet. https://www.opendoor.com/w/blog/improvements-that-increase-home-value#:~:text=Should%20I%20add%20another%20bathroom,shower%2C%20sink%2C%20and%20toilet.

Marquit. (2022, April 19). *5 types of mortgage loans for homebuyers.* Https://Www.Msn.Com/En-Us/Money/Realestate/5%20-types%20of%20mortgage%20loans%20%20homebuyers/Ar-BB1cuSxl. Retrieved June 28, 2022, from https://www.msn.com/en-us/money/realestate/5%20types%20of%20mortgage%20loans%20%20homebuyers/ar-BB1cuSxl

Mcwhinney. (2022, May 17). Fixed-rate vs adjustable rate mortgages what's the difference. Https://Www.Investopedia.Com/Mortgage/Mortgage-Rates/Fixed-versus-Adjustable-Rate/.https://www.investopedia.com/mortgage/mortgage-rates/fixed-versus-adjustable-rate/

Moving Day Etiquette: 10 Things Movers Want You to Know. (n.d.). Https://Blog.Unpakt.Com/Moving-Day-Etiquette-10-Things-Movers-Want-Know/.https://blog.unpakt.com/moving-day-etiquette-10-things-movers-want-know/

Phillips And Milbrand. (2022, May 22). *18 Moving and Packing Tips for Your Smoothest Move yet*. Https://Www.Realsimple.Com/Home-Organizing/Organizing/Moving/Moving-Packing-Tips. https://www.realsimple.com/home-organizing/organizing/moving/moving-packing-tips

Quist. (2021, October 16). *Why you should consider a multi-family property as a first-time homebuyer*. Https://Www.Newcastle.Loans/Mortgage-Guide/First-Time-Homebuyer-Multi-Family-home#A3. Retrieved June 27, 2022, from https://www.newcastle.loans/mortgage-guide/first-time-homebuyer-multi-family-home#A3

Ramsey Solutions. (2022, April 8). *2022 Home Prices: What you need to know*. Https://Www.Ramseysolutions.Com/Real-Estate/Housing-Trends. https://www.ramseysolutions.com/real-estate/housing-trends

Randall, B. (2016). Are there really too many home buyers and not enough listings? The Enterprise, 45(41), F3.

Community Property With Right Of Survivorship | Rocket Mortgage. https://www.rocketmortgage.com/learn/community-property-with-right-of-survivorship

Rent vs buy - what's right for you? (n.d.). Www.Nerdwallet.Com. https://www.nerdwallet.com/mortgages/rent-vs-buy-calculator

Reynolds. (2021, December 22). *Home Warranty Cost - 2022 Plans and Coverage*.Https://Housemethod.Com/Home-Warranty/Home-Warranty-Cost/#:~:text=A%20one%2Dyear%20home%20warranty,A%20home's%20systems%20and%20appliances. https://housemethod.com/home-warranty/home-warranty-cost/#:~:text=A%20one%2Dyear%20home%20warranty,a%20home's%20systems%20and%20appliances.

Rohde. (2022b, April 6). *A breakdown of 2022 property tax by state* [Chart]. A Breakdown of 2022 Property Tax by State. https://learn.roofstock.com/blog/property-tax-by-state

Settembre, J. (2022, February 19). *Rent Prices Surge Nationwide, Jumping More Than 50% in This Popular City*. Real Estate News & Insights | Realtor.Com®. https://www.realtor.com/news/real-estate-news/rent-prices-surge-nationwide-jumping-50-in-this-popular-city/

Short. (2022, June 8). *VA Renovation Loan 2022 How it works and where to get one.* Https://Www.Militaryvaloan.Com/Blog/What-Is-the-va-Renovation-Loan/. https://www.militaryvaloan.com/blog/what-is-the-va-renovation-loan/

Should I Rent or Buy a House? (2022, May 17). Ramseysolutions.Com. https://www.ramseysolutions.com/real-estate/buy-vs-rent-myths-busted

Simmons. (2022, May 3). *First Quarter of 2022 brings double-digit price appreciation for 70% of metros.* Https://Www.Nar.Realtor/News-room/First-Quarter-of-2022-Brings-Double-Digit-Price-Appreci-ation-for-70-of-Metros. https://www.nar.realtor/newsroom/first-quarter-of-2022-brings-double-digit-price-appreciation-for-70-of-metros

Taylor. (n.d.). *13 Signs Your Home Has Good Resale Value.* Bobvila.Com/Slideshow/13-Signs-Your-Home-Has-Good-Resale-Value-53169. https://www.bobvila.com/slideshow/13-signs-your-home-has-good-resale-value-53169

Types of Vesting Related to Real Estate Ownership. (2015, February 16). Https://Www.Deeds.Com/Articles/Types-of-Vesting-Related-to-Real-Estate-Ownership/.https://www.deeds.com/articles/types-of-vesting-related-to-real-estate-ownership/

Vermeer And Loughead. (2022, February 15). *State Individual Income Tax Rates and Brackets for 2022* [Illustration]. State Individual Income

Tax Rates and Brackets for 2022. https://taxfoundation.org/publica tions/state-individual-income-tax-rates-and-brackets/

Warden. (2021, November 30). *Average down payment on a house and when to put down more or less.* Https://Themortgagereports.-Com/60543/Average-down-Payment-on-a-House-and-Low-down-Payment-Benefits. https://themortgagereports.com/60543/average-down-payment-on-a-house-and-low-down-payment-benefits

What does holding title actually mean. (n.d.). Https://Www.Ocrealestateguy.Com/What-Does-Holding-Title-Actually-Mean/. https://www.ocrealestateguy.com/what-does-holding-title-actu ally-mean/

What is labour market information? Do I Need it? (2021, June 23). Https://Settlement.Org/Ontario/Employment/Find-a- Job/Labour-Market-Information/What-Is-Labour-Market-Infor- mation-Do-i-Need-It/. Retrieved June 28, 2022, from

Zebra. (2021, July 6). *10 of the most expensive home repairs (and how to preventthem).*Https://Www.Thezebra.Com/Resources/Home/Most-Expensive-Home-Repairs-Prevention/. https://www.thezebra.com/resources/home/most-expensive-home-repairs-prevention/

Printed in Great Britain
by Amazon

22832580R00106